T0162812

STANDING UP FOR JUSTICE

THE EMMETT TILL MURDER TRIAL

Walter Williams, Jr.

authorHOUSE®

AuthorHouse™
1663 Liberty Drive
Bloomington, IN 47403
www.authorhouse.com
Phone: 1-800-839-8640

First published by AuthorHouse 8/26/2011

ISBN: 978-1-4634-3742-8 (e)
ISBN: 978-1-4634-3744-2 (sc)

Library of Congress Control Number: 2011912508

Printed in the United States of America

Any people depicted in stock imagery provided by Thinkstock are models, and such images are being used for illustrative purposes only. Certain stock imagery © Thinkstock.

This book is printed on acid-free paper.

CHAPTER 1

The usual reasons for murder in 1955 in Mississippi against Negroes ranged from stealing food to talking back to a white person. The latest victim was a fourteen-year-old boy named Emmett Till. His murder was different for many reasons. It made the front page on virtually every newspaper in the nation.

It is September 20, 1955, inside of the Emmett Till murder trial that took place in the Mississippi delta town of Sumner. It is segregated, of course, with an all-white male jury. White press and Negro press were there, along with the secretary for the National Association for the Advancement of Colored People (NAACP), Medgar Evers.

Emmett's murder was brutal, and all the more threatening as the word spread throughout the Negro community: keep your mouth shut. But three witnesses did not let threats and intimidation prevent them from standing up and telling the truth.

The murder trial is getting ready, in its fifth and final day. The small courtroom is a suffocating 99N F., and only the white people are sipping on ice water. Others fan themselves with paper fans, trying to cool off from the hot, humid air that feels like a sweat box inside the courtroom. The atmosphere was just like a circus, the two defendants are sitting up, eating ice cream cones and playing with their children, just like they were at a picnic. It was crammed inside with 400 people—no air-conditioning—in this chamber designed only for 220. An overflow mixed crowd of nearly a thousand is waiting outside on the courthouse lawn to receive regular updates on the trial. Most Negroes are wondering if justice could ever be done in one of the most notoriously racist states in America.

The bailiff walks up in front of the jam-packed courtroom. He is a tall, white man with a receding hair line and missing four of his front teeth. The twelve all-white male jurors are wearing white, baggy, short-sleeved shirts, tan slacks, black shoes, and white straw-brimmed hats. It is 1:15 P.M.

"All rise!" the bailiff yells across the courtroom. Everyone immediately stands straight up. "Court is now in session. Your Honorable Judge Curtis M. Swango presiding."

The Judge walks over to his desk. He is a silver-haired middle-aged white man wearing a tan brown suit and tie. He sits down at his chair in front of his desk, and everyone sits down right after him. The bailiff clears his throat before he speaks again.

"This is the murder trial of Emmett Louis Till. The two defendants, Mr. Roy Bryant and Mr. J. W. Milam, is accused of first degree murder!"

"Is the district attorney ready to cross-examine his first witness?" the Judge asks.

Mr. Chatham, from Chicago, a tall, dark-haired man wearing a long-sleeved white shirt, gray slacks, and a gray tie, stands up from the prosecutor's table. He approaches the bench like he is on a very important mission. He stands in front of the courtroom. "Yes your Honor," the slender attorney responds. "The State calls on Curtis Jones!"

A dark-skinned Negro boy who looks like he is in his late teens stands up. He is as nervous as a cat trapped inside of a dog pound. He quickly walks up to the witness stand.

"Place your right hand up," the toothless bailiff shouts.

The terrified young boy places his left hand on the Bible, then raises his right hand that is shaking out of control.

"Do you swear to tell the truth and nothing but the truth so help you God?"

"Yes, sir, I do," Curtis says in a low-pitched tone.

"Speak up, boy!" the bailiff roars at him.

"Yes, sir, I do," he repeats in a much clearer voice.

"Then take a seat!"

Curtis sits down in the witness chair. The district attorney walks up to the youth.

"Could you state your full name for the court?"

"C-Curtis Lee J-Jones," he stutters.

"Could you tell the court who Emmett Till was to you?"

"He was my cousin. We both came down here together from Chicago. Most of the kids back home used to call him Bobo. That was his nickname."

"What kind of kid was Bobo?"

"Well, he love pulling pranks. He was always messing around like that."

"So he just loved to kid around like most kids his age do, and he pulled one of his pranks Wednesday evening on August at the grocery and meat market store, is that correct?"

"Yes, sir," Curtis answers quickly.

"Tell the court exactly what happened that Wednesday at 7:30 P.M. on August the twenty-fourth."

"Well, I snuck my grandfather's '41 Ford while he was giving a sermon at church. Then Bobo and my other cousin, Maurice, went to

Bryant Grocery Store. There we met up with one other kid, then I began a game of checkers with an old man sitting by the side of the store."

"And what was young Emmett doing?"

All of a sudden Curtis is sweating, like he had just run up a steep hill, ignoring the lawyer's question with his silence.

The attorney gently rubs his chin and looks the witness directly in the eyes. In a very forceful voice, he asks, "Mr. Jones, what was Emmett doing while you were playing checkers with this old man?"

The Negro boy takes a couple of swallows and waits a while before answering. "Bobo was showing off some pictures of a white girl who he knew back in Chicago. He bragged to the other kids that this w-white g-girl was his g-g-girlfriend."

Curtis's head is hanging down the entire time he is speaking. All of the whites murmur out loud of their disapproval, but Curtis continues. "Maurice told Bobo that there is a white girl inside the store and dared Bobo to go in there to talk to her."

"And what did young Emmett do when his cousin dared him to do this?"

Curtis starts trembling even more when he begins to answer the attorney's next question. "He went inside the store to buy some candy. When he was leaving out of the store, he said to the white woman, 'Bye-bye, baby!'"

The murmur of the whites grows even louder this time inside of the hot, stuffy courtroom.

"Who was this white woman to whom he said 'Bye-bye, baby!'?"

"Mrs. Bryant."

"That would be the wife of the defendant, Roy Bryant, is that correct?"

"Yes, sir."

"Go on. What happened next after that remark was made?"

"The old man that I was playing checkers with starting telling us that she would go to her car and get a pistol and blow Bobo's brains out. After he said that to us, we all jumped inside the car. When Mrs. Bryant came out of the swinging screen door, we sped out of that town as fast as we could."

"And by the next day the incident had become a good story for you, Maurice, and young Emmett maybe to laugh about years later, but the talk went beyond just you three boys. A girl who had heard it through the grapevine said when that lady's husband came back, there was going to be big trouble. Roy Bryant was out of town at the time trucking shrimp from Louisiana to Texas. You or Emmett did not know of this at the time, did you?"

"No, sir."

"I was told that Maurice resented Emmett's fancy Chicago ways and told Bryant all about the incident between his cousin and Bryant's wife."

"Yes, Maurice did that," Curtis says, with disappointment on his face.

"Did you also know Mrs. Bryant was not going to tell her husband about what Emmett did, fearing that he may overreact?"

"No, sir, I was not aware of that at all."

The slender district attorney reaches into his front pocket and pulls out a white handkerchief. "What about your grandfather? Did he know what Emmett did that day?" he asks, wiping the sweat that was pouring from the back of his neck.

"No sir."

"Now tell us exactly what happened that night when Roy Bryant and J. W. Milam arrived at your grandfather's cabin."

"Well, I could hear them talking to my grandfather at the front porch. Mr. Milam and Mr. Bryant was talking very loud that night."

Curtis starts at the very beginning telling his story about the kidnapping of his cousin, Emmett Till.

It was eleven o'clock. Milam and Bryant were talking to Mose Wright, an elderly bald dark Negro man wearing blue overalls. "Can I help you, gentlemen?" Mose asked politely.

Bryant, a white male with thick, dark hair and dark, bushy eyebrows, said sternly, "Look, preacher, I heard that you have a couple of Nigras from out of Chicago staying here with ya."

"Yes, suh, they staying here for a few weeks. Is there anything wrong, suh?"

"We want to see the Nigra who done all that talk."

"Suh, I don't know anything about that."

"Well I do!" Bryant yelled. "One of those Nigras in there sass at my wife!"

"The two boys that staying here with me would never do nothing that stupid!" he said.

"Oh yeah?" The six-foot-four-inch Milam interrupted, in his thick Mississippi accent. "I thought all you dirty niggers were stupid!" he said, holding a pistol in his right hand and a flashlight in his left.

"Not stupid enough to do something like that, suh."

"Then you better ask whatever God that you pray to that they didn't. 'Cause we about to ask them ourself!"

"Suh, can you please ask them tomorrow? They sleeping pretty hard tonight."

"You must of been drinking moonshine tonight, boy!"

"Preacher, do you know how far we come to get here? We seeing those Nigras tonight!" Bryant demanded.

Mose's voice started to shake. "Suh, I understand all these things that ya telling me, but my nephew and grandson would never sass any white women."

"Are you calling me a liar, Preacher?"

"Naw, suh, naw, suh!"

"What is these two niggers' names that is staying here with ya?" Milam growled.

"Emmett is my nephew and Curtis is my grandson."

Milam shouted. "I didn't ask you who they were to you, I just ask you to tell us what their names were!"

"Sorry, suh."

"You better be."

"Well, one of your kinfolk is coming with us tonight, Preacher." Bryant warned him.

"Are you gonna hurt one of them, suh?"

"It all depends on how they answer our question," Milam said, with a devilish grin.

"They only just kids, suh."

"I don't give a shit what they are, one of those black bastards whistled at this man's wife." Milam pointed at Bryant. "And my sister-in-law!"

"Believe me, Preacher, one of those Nigras in there gonna get exactly what he deserve," Bryant snickered.

"You really believe one of the boys whistled at your wife, suh?"

"I am about to lose my patience with you, boy. My wife said some Nigra that she never seen before call her Baby and whistle at her in my store while she was working, and my wife ain't no liar, either!"

"But suh, how do you know that it was Emmett or Curtis? It could of been anybody."

"Because any Nigra from down here would know better to act that way towards a white woman. Now shut up with all your questions!"

Milam pushed Mose out of the way. "Now step aside, boy!"

"When you come in. Can you just talk to them please, suh?"

Milam laughed out loud. "This old coon really must of been drinking moonshine tonight."

"We ain't making no promises," Bryant said in a sharp tone.

Milam added, "Especially to the likes of you!"

"You know, I just remember the boys ain't here tonight," Mose said.

Milam burst out, "Who do you think we are, a couple of dumb rednecks? Well, do you, nigger!"

"Naw, suh, it just occur to me that the boys ain't here, that's all."

Bryant stared at Mose for a few seconds. "Oh, it just occur to you, huh. Don't lie to us, because if you do, we may have to teach you a lesson, too."

"Now are they in there, yes or no?!" screamed Milam.

"Yas, suh, they here." Mose admitted, hanging his head down.

Milam pressed his pistol on the side of Mose's nose and cocked the trigger back. "If you every try to lie to us again, I will blow your goddamn nose off your face, do you understand me, boy?!"

"Yas, suh!"

"Now show us where they is," Milam ordered.

Mose walked inside his cabin. Bryant and Milam followed him into a tiny, dark bedroom. Milam walked up to three boys that were all lying in a small bed. He shined his flashlight in their faces.

"Who did that talking at a white woman in the grocery store four days ago?"

"I did," Emmett said, with no fear.

Curtis and Maurice, lying next to Emmett, raised their heads up, trying to take a peek at the imposing 270-pound white man, whose gut hung over his jeans.

CHAPTER 2

"Put your heads back down before I snap them off!" Milam shouted, twisting his pink lips. The two boys tucked their head down underneath the covers quickly.

Milam then shined his flashlight down only on Emmett's face. "Roy!" he yelled at the top of his lungs, while giving Emmett an evil glare. Bryant rushed up to his half-brother, wondering what he was so excited about.

Milam waved his flashlight towards Emmett. "This is the one who sass Carolyn, and get this! The damn fool admitted it."

"He what!" Bryant raged. He snatched the .45-caliber pistol out of Milam's hand and pressed it against Emmett's forehead.

Bryant looked him in the eyes. "I will blow your head clean off. Now get some clothes on!"

The young youth was wearing only his underwear. He put on a shirt and pants, then reached for some socks.

"What are you slowing around for, coon? Hurry it up!" Bryant yelled.

"I have to put my socks on, don't I?" Emmett snapped back.

Milam's whole face turned into a frown. "You can sho' tell that this nigger ain't from around here."

Bryant began to pull the trigger, the gun was still pressed up against Emmett's forehead. Bryant's eyes were dead, and the only thing on his mind that very moment was killing the smart-mouthed Negro boy. "Bye-bye, nigger!"

Mose's heart was beating like a bongo drum. "Mr. Bryant, please don't kill 'em. I beg of you. He ain't got good sense. He don't know any better. This is only his second time down here in Mississippi!"

"I don't care how many times he's been down here. Ain't no nigger gonna sass me like that!"

"He's from up North. He really don't know a thang about how to act around white folk down South. He's only just fourteen years old. Why not give the boy a good whumping and leave it at that!"

"How old are you?" Milam asked Mose in a vicious tone.

"I am sixty-four years old, suh," he stuttered.

"If you cause any trouble, you'll never live to see sixty-five!"

Just seconds later, Mose's wife walked into the bedroom with pink curlers in her hair, barefooted, wearing a long white cotton robe. Mrs. Wright was nice-looking for a woman of her age. She wiped her eyes with the back of her hand and couldn't believe what she was seeing. "I don't know what's going on, but whatever it is, me and my husband will pay you whatever you want just to leave us alone!"

Bryant stared at the woman and paused a few seconds. He was thinking about taking the money, depending on how much they were willing to pay them. But Milam picked up on that and made it very clear who was really in charge.

"We ain't taking no money!" Milam shouted. "Now you get back in your bedroom before I put a bullet in your black ass!"

Mrs. Wright had no choice but to listen to the evil intruders. She sadly walked out of the room.

Mose turned to the two angry men and pleaded with them. "Suh, he's just only fourteen years old! He just turn fourteen. Don't take 'em!"

"I don't care how old he is," Milam snarled. He shouldn't of done what he done."

Emmett turned to look over at his terrified uncle. "Don't worry, Uncle Mose. I'll be okay."

Milam grabbed Emmett roughly from the back of his neck and pushed him towards the living room. Mose walked behind them.

Milam smirked at Emmett, "We gonna teach you a lesson that you ain't never gonna forget, boy."

"Yeah, you should of stay up North," Bryant said, pointing the pistol in Emmett's back, nudging him up to the front door.

"Are you gonna bring the boy back?" Mose asked nervously.

Milam gave the old man a long, hateful glare. "Like I said before, if you want to live to be sixty-five, you keep your black lips shut about us ever being here."

Bryant, Milam, and Emmett all walked out. Milam shut the door behind them.

Just seconds later, Mrs. Wright walked into the living room. "I heard the door slam, so I figger they must be gone now."

"Yeah, they gone all right," Moses said.

"Where is Bobo?"

"They done took him away."

"Why?"

"They said he done whistle at a white woman. Bryant's wife."

"Lord have mercy, I just knew that boy's sharp tongue would get him in a whole mess of trouble. I just pray that they don't beat him too bad."

"Oh, they gonna do more than just beat on him."

"How do you know?"

"'Cause I could see it in their eyes!"

"No! He just fourteen. Do they know that Bobo is just only fourteen years old?"

"I told them how old Bobo is. They don't care. The only thing they care about is that he got fresh with a white woman and that it is their duty as white men to teach the boy a good lesson. And believe me, they gonna!"

Inside the courtroom, Curtis is done giving his testimony.

"Thank you for providing us with that great testimony. There will be no further questions, your Honor."

"You may step down," Judge Swango adds.

The nervous teen steps down from the witness stand. When he approaches his seat, all the whites turn their heads and give him mean stares until he sits down. Some continue to stare at him.

"Your Honor, I would like to call on the next witness."

"Then do it!" Judge Swango snaps.

The attorney looks toward the back of the courtroom. "Levy Collins, would you please step up to the witness stand?!" He shouts.

A Negro man in his early twenties comes through the back of the courtroom door wearing a tight white T-shirt, ripped up blue jeans torn from the knees, and tennis shoes with holes in them. He walks up to the witness stand and stands in front of the bailiff.

"Right hand up, left hand on the Bible."

The young man does exactly what he is told.

"Do you swear to tell the truth and nothing but the truth, so help you God?"

"Yas, suh."

"Sit down."

Levy sits down with a frightened look on his face. The district attorney walks up to the witness, "Where do you live, Mr. Collins?"

"I live in Glendora. It's in Sunflower County in Mis'sippi, suh."

"Do you have a family?"

"I have a family. I have a wife and four children, suh."

"Where are your wife and children?"

"They is in Glendora, suh."

"Have you read in the daily papers about the death of Emmett Till who was killed here in Mississippi?"

"I can't read, but I heard lots of talk."

"Are you employed, Mr. Collins?"

"Employed?" he asks with a puzzled expression.

"Are you working, Mr. Collins?"

"Yas, suh."

"Were you working for J. W. Milam?"

"Yas, suh."

"What kind of work did you do for him?"

"I run the cotton picker."

"How long have you been working for J. W. Milam?"

"About four years, suh."

The attorney stares down at the witness for a few seconds, and gave him a sad glare. "Do you even understand that Milam needs brawn and very little brains and he helps to see to it that he has an abundance of workers who fit into this category, and that is you, Mr Collins? In other words, he is taking advantage of you."

"Mr. Milam won't do that to me. He's my friend."

"Yeah right," he said with a light laugh. "Do you know the other defendant, Roy Bryant?"

"Yas, suh."

"How?"

"Through Mr. Milam."

"What time did you get off from work on August 28th?"

"About 11:30 P.M."

"Do you know that there is a witness that claims he seen you and another Negro three hours later after that time with Roy Bryant, J. W. Milam, and Emmett Till, when he was very much alive, inside the back of a 1955 green Chevy pickup truck by the Tallahatchie River, where eventually Emmett's body was later found?"

Both of Levy's knees are trembling like crazy. He begins to bite his fingernails. "Naw, suh, n-no one s-saw m-me. I went home right after work."

"Do you know a Negro man by the name of Willie Loggins?"

The pleasant looking man jerks his head up nervously. "Yas, suh," he says reluctantly.

"How long have you know Mr. Loggins?"

"At least over fourteen years. We grew up together."

"Were you and Mr. Loggins together on August 28, Sunday morning?"

"Yas, suh, just for a little while."

"What did you and Mr. Loggins do that night? Did you go out drinking?"

"I don't drink and he don't drink."

"Are you really trying to sit there and tell everyone in this courtroom that you don't drink? Come on, Mr. Collins, you can do better than that. So you didn't drink at all that night?"

"I drank a little beer but not a whole lot. Then we went to Greenwood to see some girls after work." He pauses for a few seconds. "Oops." Levy quickly covers his hands over his mouth.

"Trust me, Mr. Collins," the attorney says. "No one in this courtroom is the least bit interested in your infidelity." He pauses, then continues talking. "So if you saw these girls after work, and you say that you get off at 11:30 P.M., it had to be midnight when you finally met up with them, correct?"

"Yas, suh."

"What were the girls' names?"

"I don't know."

"You don't even know the names of the girls that you went to see. You have to be lying or you had to be really hammered, Mr. Collins."

"Naw, suh, I just don't recall their names, that's all."

"When you and Mr. Loggins went to see these girls, how did you make it back home?"

"Willie brought me back in his car and let me out at my house, and that was the last that I saw of him."

"Mr. Collins, why don't you just admit to the people in this courtroom that on that Sunday morning you and Mr. Loggins were with J. W. Milam and Roy Bryant when they murdered this fourteen-year-old boy. Then you and Willie Loggins cleaned up the blood inside of the pickup truck just seconds after his young life was taken from him!"

"Naw suh, we was with some girls that day, as God is my witness," he pleads.

"Where do these so-called girls live?" The attorney asks with an unconvincing smile on his face.

"They live on Johnson Street."

"Johnson and what?"

"I don't know." Levy shrugs his shoulders. "Just on Johnson Street, suh."

The six-foot-one-inch attorney pushes his straight black hair out of his eyes and says in a very forceful voice, "You know, your story has more holes in it than a block of Swiss cheese. Let me tell everyone here the real story on what really happened on that Sunday morning, August 28, as it was told to me by your childhood friend, Willie Loggins, who I spoke with on the phone just yesterday."

The attorney begins telling everyone in the courtroom how Willie and Levy met up with Milam and Bryant.

It was one of the hottest, humid nights in Mississippi. Both men were sipping on some bottles of R-C Colas.

"It sho' feel good to be just getting off of work. I just wish it wasn't so hot, though," Willie said in a funny Southern accent. He was a brown-complected Negro with bright brown eyes and a flat nose.

Levy wiped the sweat from his neck. "It just as hot at night as it is in the daytime."

Willie quickly went to another subject. "Hey, did you hear about that Chicago Negro whistling at a white woman?"

"Yeah, I heard about that alright."

"That boy must of been out of his fool mind."

"What do you think would make a Negro do something like that?"

"Some of those Northern Negroes can be kind of cocky sometimes," Willie said.

"At this point I don't care. Even Northern Negroes should still know better to whistle at a white woman down here in the South."

"I heard that he was only a fourteen-year-old boy," Willie said with some sympathy.

"That young, huh? Well, he still should of known better."

"What do you think they do to him if they catch 'em?"

"Probably put a good scare in him, that's all," Levy assumed.

"You don't think they do more than that?"

"If he had been a grown man and did that, they probably string 'em up."

"I don't know, Levy. Flirting with a white woman down here is a serious thang to be doing for a Negro, no matter what age they is. And don't you know the white woman's husband?"

"I sho' do, and I know his half-brother, too. His name is J. W. Milam, and he's a big bald mean cracker."

Just talking about this white man set Levy's teeth on edge. "And let me tell you one thang else about this cracker. Killing a Negro for him is like killing a cockroach. Easy!"

"Well, in that case, I sho' don't wanna be that boy right about now," Levy replied in a nervous voice.

"You and me both, because if there is any two rednecks that I would never ever want to cross in my life, that would be Bryant and Milam. But especially Milam!"

Willie turned his head and spotted two white men walking across the street, heading towards them with smug looks on their faces. "There's two white men coming this way, and they don't look very friendly!"

"Have you ever seen any white man in the South that look friendly?" Levi asked, as he turned his head to take a look at the two perpetrators coming across the street. They smelled like they had been drinking hard alcohol all that day. All of a sudden, Levy became sick to his stomach, and his eyes bulged out of his head.

Willie looked at his childhood friend, then he began to panic. "What's wrong?" he asked.

"Here come trouble, and I do mean trouble," he said in a shaking voice.

Milam and Bryant walked up to the two Negroes.

"Hey, Collins, what you two niggers up to?" Milam said, with an ugly grin.

Levy just smiled politely. "Just enjoying this nice weather that we having tonight, Mr. Milam."

"We need ya'll to do something for us."

"Sho, we can. Anything you want, Mr. Bryant," Levy said grinning, nodding his head back and forth, showing all his white teeth.

"Ya'll heard about that city Nigra who whistle at my wife?"

"Yas, suh, we were just talking about how foolish that was, wasn't we, Willie."

"We sho' was."

"You were, huh?" Milam said in a sly tone. "Well, we got the little monkey in the back of my truck, and we taught him a real good lesson about getting fresh with white women down here. We want ya'll to clean up the blood inside of the truck."

Willie was scared out of his mind. He didn't forget what Levy just had told him about the two white men, especially the big bald one, who looked like a mean old bulldog in the face. He didn't want to get mixed up in no funny business, and he was going to try to avoid it if he could. "If you don't mind, suh, we rather not," he said in a broken tone.

"What did you say, nigger?!" Milam's booming voice made Willie almost jump out of his skin.

"He didn't mean nothing, honest. We be mighty glad to help you, Mr. Milam and Mr. Bryant, mighty glad," Levy whined.

Milam put both hands on his hips and glared down at Levy and Willie. "Then you better get off your black asses and come with us. Leave those soda bottles. I don't want no drinking in my truck."

The two Negroes put down their colas and followed them to a big green pickup truck.

CHAPTER 3

"Get in the back," Milam told them.

"What else do we have to do after we done cleaning up the blood, suh?" Willie asked.

"Don't worry about that. Just do whatever you are told, boy!"

"Get in the back like J. W. told ya!" Bryant ordered Willie.

Levy and Willie climbed into the back of the truck. Inside was someone lying in the corner, covered all over in blood. Willie gasped at what he saw, then pointed at the bloody individual. "What's that?"

Milam roared, "Goddamn you, boy. You ask a lot of questions!"

"Hush up, Willie," Levy said very quickly.

"It's that Chicago nigger," Bryant answered smartly. "And ya'll gonna help us clean up this mess and bury the body. And if you tell anyone, you two will be buried right beside him."

"And it's not a threat, it's a promise!" Milam shouted.

Then, the two kidnappers, walked away and went inside of the truck. Milam sat in the driver seat, and Bryant climbed into the passenger seat. They drove off and headed through a long, narrow, dark cotton field.

"I don't feel good about this. Not one damn bit," Willie protested, sitting on the edge of the moving truck.

"I don't either, but when we were asked to help, I didn't expect anything like this to happen."

"First of all we wasn't ask nothing. Those rednecks didn't give us much of a choice!"

"Lower your voice before they hear you up there," Levy whispered.

"I don't want to go down for no murder rap, Levy."

"We didn't murder nobody."

Suddenly Emmett rose up and reached out both arms towards the two nervous men. "Help me, please!" he said in a strained voice. Emmett looked glassy-eyed, like he just came out of a bad dream.

"Oh shit!" Willie screamed like a school girl. He jumped so high, he almost fell out of the moving truck.

"Oh Lord, this boy is still alive. What do we do now?!" Levy hollered.

"I don't know maybe we should just jump off this truck and run like hell!"

"If we do, we will prob'ly be looking just like him. We may all go to jail now if this boy die on us."

"We all! Those crackers up there," Willie whispered, "ain't spending one second in a jail cell for killing this boy."

"You really think so?"

"Don't nobody gives a damn about any white man killing no Negro. It happens all the time down here. If anybody may go to jail for this, it will be us, not them."

"Please help me!" Emmett pleaded again, this time in a low-pitched sound.

"Shut up," Levy said, with plenty of anger. "This is all your fault anyway. You should of knew better in the first place to whistle at a white woman."

Milam shouted from the front of the truck, out the side window, "What are you two yapping about back there?!"

"This Negro boy back here is still alive, suh!" Levy yelled back.

"That's impossible. We took turns beating on him. There is no way that he should still be alive. Not after the ass-whipping we put on that nigger!"

"Come see for yourself, suh."

Milam parked over to the side of a deserted pitch-dark road. The two thugs rushed up to the back of the truck. Emmett was on his hands and knees.

"I'll be damned!" Milam said. "That som-bitch is still alive."

"That is one tough-skin nigger, I tell you that," Bryant claimed. "We had to be beating on him for at least a whole sixty seconds."

Milam walked up to Emmett, who was still on his hands and knees. He pulled out his .45 pistol and stuck it on the top of the youth's head. "I bet ya he ain't tougher than a bullet!"

Willie interrupted. "Mr. Bryant and Mr. Milam?"

"What is your problem, boy?!" Milam screamed.

"I just want to go home!" Willie cried.

"Don't tell me you chickening out on us."

"Mr. Milam, I just don't want to have nothing to do with this anymore."

"Neither do I, suh," Levy added.

Bryant's pale blue eyes aimed towards Levy like a red spotlight. "You ain't bailing out on us, Collins!"

Milam then aimed his gun in the direction of the two Negroes.

"Mr. Milam, don't shoot. I got a wife and kids. Please, suh, don't shoot me!" Levy begged.

"Shut your mouth up. The both of you better not even think about jumping off this goddamn truck and running away, 'cause if you do, I will hunt you down like a dog and blow both of your brains out!"

The two men's hearts froze, and all they could do was look helplessly at the gun that was pointed at them. They were genuinely afraid, no question of that. Almost blind with fear.

Milam moved the gun away from Levy and Willie, then aimed it back towards Emmett. He reached into his front pocket with his free hand, pulled out a cigarette, shoved it in his mouth, and lit it with a small lighter. He took one long drag, blew cigarette smoke out of both nostrils, and flicked his cigarette into the grass.

"Let's get out of here," Milam said eagerly. He glared at Emmett, Willie, and Levy with his big, reddish eyes. Just seconds later, they all got into the green pickup truck and drove away.

The district attorney clears his throat, then turns to face the man on the witness stand. "Now that is what I was told really happened after you got off from work on August the twenty-eighth, the story I just told. Did it happen that way, Mr. Levy Collins?"

"Naw, suh. That story is not true at all," he says in a quick panic.

"Then you tell me if this is true. Did your childhood friend, Willie Loggins, leave Mississippi on August the twenty-ninth, just one day after Emmett was murdered?"

"Yas, suh, that is true, but—"

Before the witness can get another word in, the attorney quickly cuts him off.

"Where did he go?"

"He went to St. Louis, and I told him to send back after me," Levi answers in a hurry.

"What do you mean, 'send back after you'?" the attorney shoots right back.

"I mean send me a ticket to St. Louis," he tries to say with an innocent-looking face.

"So you wanted to leave Mississippi, too?"

"Nah, suh!"

"Then why did you want Mr. Loggins to send you a ticket to St. Louis if you didn't want to leave Mississippi?"

"I don't know, suh," he says, both knees knocking together.

The attorney opens his eyes wide and scratches the back of his head. "You are a grown man and you don't know why you wanted Mr. Loggins to send you a ticket to St. Louis. Well, I know why, because you are feeling guilty about you and Willie Loggins helping the two defendants, Roy Bryant and J. W. Milam, get rid of Emmett's corpse. And the reason why your childhood pal left the next day after Emmett's murder he was just so scared out of his wits of Milam, that he fled to another state."

He pauses for a brief moment, showing some sympathy towards the frightened man. "Look, Mr. Collins, I know that you are afraid, but why don't you just do the decent thing and admit that you and Mr. Loggins were with Roy Bryant and J. W. Milam in back of a green pickup truck with Emmett when he was half dead and beat up to a bloody pulp."

"I don't know anything about that, suh!" Levy says, with a weary look.

The attorney rolls his eyes in frustration. "Mr. Collins, nothing you have said today adds up to anything or makes any kind of sense at all. I hope that the jury will recognize that you know a lot more than you are revealing on this witness stand. I believe just your testimony alone exposes you as a big liar, Mr. Collins."

He turns towards the judge. "No further questions, your Honor!" The district attorney says in a loud voice, then returns to his seat.

Levy steps down. The defense attorney, Mr. Carleton, seated at the defense table next to Bryant, Milam, and their wives, stands up and strolls across the courtroom. He's a short, pudgy white man with red curly hair, and he's wearing a white suit. He stands in front of the courtroom with a smirk on his face. "Will the boy's mama come up here!" he announces.

Miss Bradley has silky jet-black hair, dark brown eyes, and creamy brown skin. She's absolutely gorgeous, wearing a swirly dress with large splashes of bright colors, which looks dramatic against her brown skin.

A hush falls over the courtroom when the defense attorney rudely calls her up to the stand. It is clear to everyone by Miss Bradley's demeanor that she will not be intimidated, even though most white spectators resent her presence at the trial. She displays an air of confidence and determination as she walks up to the witness stand.

"Sit down," the chubby attorney says with a mean voice.

Miss Bradley takes her seat facing the two men who are accused of murdering her son. Milam and Bryant are surrounded by their family and supporters. The two men start to ignore her as the defense attorney begins his questioning.

"Be honest with yourself. You don't really know if the body that was taken from out of the river is your boy, now do you, Mamie?!" he yells in her face.

"I knew it was my son. He was wearing a ring that belonged to my deceased husband, who died in the war fighting for this country!"

"That will be quite enough of that, Miss Bradley," the Judge shouts. "Counsel did not ask you anything about your dead husband fighting for this country. Just answer the question, is that clear?"

"Yes, sir."

The curly-haired attorney smiles at the Judge and says, "Thank you, your Honor." He pauses for a brief moment. "So, are you telling this court that the only way that you could identify the body was because of some stupid ring that your dead husband used to own?"

Miss Bradley turns to the all-white male jury and tries to reach them. "It wasn't just only the ring. When my son's body was shipped home to Chicago, I finally was able to lay my eyes on him. I began to examine his feet, teeth, and gums and hair. A mother knows her own child. I known him since he was born. I just looked at him very carefully and I was able to find out that it was my son, Emmett Louis Till, beyond a shadow of a doubt!"

The defense attorney rushes up to the defense table with a scowl look on his face. He picks up a large photograph and walks in front of Miss Bradley. "This is a photograph of the disfigured corpse seconds after being brought out of the Tallahatchie River." He shoves the photograph up to Miss Bradley's face. "Is this your dead boy?!" he screams at her.

Miss Bradley takes the photograph, looks at it for a while. The courtroom is completely silent. She takes off her glasses, wipes her eye, and nods sadly.

"Did you collect on the policy yet?" he asked.

"No I haven't, sir."

The defense attorney reaches over towards the grieving mother and snatches the picture clean out of her hand.

"I'm not concerned about any money," she replies. "I've been waiting for Bobo's death certificate, but I never received one yet."

"And do you know why you don't have a certificate? Because no one really knows if that was your boy's body that was pulled out of the Tallahatchie River." The short attorney stands at eye level to the young mother and shouts loudly in her face. "Not even you, the boy's own mama, really knows!"

The district attorney jumps up, almost out of his seat. "Objection, your Honor," he says with urgency. "This is way out of line, the way Mr. Carleton is dealing with Miss Bradley. He has insulted her by referring to her as Mamie instead of Miss Bradley. Now he is yelling at her as if she is on trial. This poor woman has just lost her son, for God's sake." He continues with compassion, "Hasn't Miss Bradley been through enough already, your Honor?!"

Mr. Chatham slowly sits back down, the Judge pauses, folds his hands on top of his desk, and leans back. "Counsel, I am going to have to ask you to settle down some."

"Yes, your Honor," the defense attorney says with an unpleasant look. He darts his eyes at Miss Bradley like a laser beam and says angrily, "Now Mamie, did you—"

"I object!" the district attorney shouts.

"On what grounds?" Judge Swango asked, in an irritated tone.

"Your Honor, Mr. Carleton is still referring to her as Mamie instead of Miss Bradley."

"Mr. Chatham, your objection is overruled. The counsel has the God-given right to call Miss Bradley by her first name if he so wishes. This is America, you know."

"Even if it's done to belittle her?"

"You are just making assumptions at this point. Your objection is still overruled. You do not know what the counsel's intentions truly are, so stop acting like you do."

The district attorney sits down quickly, frowning. The Judge turns toward the defense attorney. "Now continue on with your cross-examination, Mr. Carleton."

"Yes, sir, your Honor." He smiles. "Now, Mamie, you really don't think that these two hard-working, fine family men really killed your boy, now do you, Mamie?" he says with a smirk.

"Yes, sir, I do," she says boldly. "They are filled with hatred that comes from fear and insecurity bred into them. My child was sweet and innocent!"

"If he was so sweet and innocent, why did he try to attack a white woman in her own store?"

"What in the world can a boy do with a full-grown woman? Look at all these white men raping Negro women and girls all the time down here in Mississippi and what has been done about that."

"That will be quite enough!" the Judge shouts. "You have said way too much already. Watch your mouth, Miss Bradley."

"Yes, sir," she says softly.

"Are you educated?" Mr. Carleton asks in a stern voice.

"Yes, sir. I may go back to college to become a teacher. I really enjoy working with children."

"Hurray for you!" he says in a condescending manner. "Now do you think just because you were lucky enough to be just one of the few Nigras with some education behind you that it gives you the right to say whatever you want in this courtroom?"

"No, sir," she says in a sharp tone. "I am just expressing my opinion. Like Judge Swango said, this is America, you know!"

The courtroom all of a sudden becomes dead silent. The defense attorney is speechless. "Right about now I wish it wasn't," he grumbles. "Did you talk to the boy about the way that he should behave down here with the white folks?"

"Yes, sir, I did."

The attorney laughs lightly and says, "Apparently not good enough!"

"So are you saying my son was murdered, sir?" Miss Bradley said in a very calm voice.

"I did not say that!!"

"You just asked me if I ever had a talk with my son about how to act with white people down here, and I said yes, and you said apparently not good enough. When you made that very hurtful statement, were you implying that my son was indeed murdered because he had gotten out of line with a white woman?"

The defense attorney's cheeks turn bright red. "Why you nig—your Honor," he says quickly. "There will be no further questions for this gal."

The dark-haired attorney stands up from the table. He walks over to the witness stand, as the defense attorney walks off talking under his breath in a rage, and sits back down in his seat.

"Miss Bradley, how did you find out that your only child was murdered?" the slender lawyer asked.

"My uncle called me in Chicago and told me what happen over the phone."

"Mose Wright is your uncle, is that correct?"

"Yes, sir."

"And Emmett's great uncle, is that correct?"

"Yes, sir."

"Is it true that when your son's distended body was pulled out from the river, it was so badly mangled that Emmett's own uncle couldn't identify the body, only by an initialed ring on his finger that belonged to your deceased husband did he really know it was Emmett?"

"Y-yes, sir."

"Are you going to be okay, Miss Bradley?"

"Yes, I will be alright," she says, wiping the tears away from her face."

"Miss Bradley, it is very important for you to really understand that some of these next questions may be difficult for you to answer. But I want everyone in this courtroom to understand the full extent of the heartache that these two defendants have put you through."

"I do understand."

"Good," he says with relief. "Now, from the information that I received, some sheriff wanted to bury the decomposing body quickly, but Mose Wright told you on the phone exactly what the sheriff was up to, and you demanded that the body not be buried but to be sent home. The sheriff had the mortician sign an order that the casket not be open, but as soon as it arrived in Chicago you decided to have an open casket funeral. Could you tell the court why did you make this bold decision, especially after knowing how disfigured your son's face looked?"

"Yes I can. I was standing in the hallway of the A. A. Rayner Funeral Home having a pleasant conversation with Mr. Rayner, the funeral director back in Chicago. He couldn't understand why on God's green earth that I would want Bobo to have an open-casket funeral either."

She begins to explain to the court the entire story.

The funeral director had a thick, dark beard. He wore small, round-shaped eyeglasses that hung from the tip of his nose and was dressed in a black suit and tie. "I can understand you being upset about what happened to your son," the funeral director said with sympathy. "Because of the awful condition of his face, I just wouldn't advise you to have a open-casket funeral. It may anger some folks around here."

CHAPTER 4

"Mr. Rayner," she said with a solemn look.

"Yes, ma'am," he answered quickly.

"I want people to be angry about what happened to my son."

"You do?" Mr. Rayner asked with a surprised look on his face.

"Yes I do. Have you ever had sent a loved one on vacation and had them returned to you in a pine box, that is so horribly battered and waterlogged someone needs to tell you that sickening sight is your loved one?"

"No, ma'am, I have not."

"I want the whole world to see what these monsters have done to my only child."

"Yes, ma'am, I can understand that, but why is the burial delayed for four days?"

"I did that because I want as many people as possible to really get a chance to see racism at the level of its full evilness. That is why I am also having a three-day viewing."

"You think that your son's appearance is a symbol of racism at its very worst?"

"Yes I do."

"Is it really true that these two white men murdered your son because he had whistled at some white woman?"

"That's what I've been told, but I don't believe that Bobo would do anything like that."

"You know, there is something very different about your son's death since his body has arrived here. Everyone just cannot stop talking about the reason why he may have been killed."

"I know, there's been cold-blooded, callous killing before in the South, but my dear Bobo! His death has touched everyone in such a way that I have never seen before."

"Your son's death has opened the eyes of so many people to the cold fact that not even a young child's life is safe when it comes to racism and hatred."

"But I just thank God that his body was found, because it was not supposed to be found at all, once it was thrown in the river. The weight of a seventy-five-pound fan that had barbed wire attached to it tied around Bobo's neck should of kept his corpse from rising back up."

"Yes, but God sure had a different plan, didn't he," the funeral director smiled.

"Yes, He sure did." Miss Bradley smiled back.

"Who was it that found your son's body anyway?"

"His body was found by a boy who was fishing. When they pulled up my son's body, his face was hacked, and I believe it wasn't by any accident."

"What do you mean, Miss Bradley?"

"The whole point I feel of killing and mutilating my son, inflicting agony on his last moments, was to prove that he was never human. When arriving at the train station where the body had to be picked up at, when I open up the casket, I collapsed on the concrete train platform and had to be taken away from the station in a wheelchair."

Mr. Rayner paused, took a long, deep breath.

"Miss Bradley, it really pains me to say this, but you need to take another look at Emmett's body one more time. I have to be certain that you know for sure that the corpse that was sent here to me is really your son."

Miss Bradley was becoming frustrated at the funeral director. "I told you already that I was a hundred percent sure that the body that I looked at today was my son. Now you are telling me I have to view his mutilated body all over again?"

"I am very sorry, Miss Bradley. Truly I am. But I have to be absolutely positive that I will not be burying the wrong body. I could be in a lot of trouble if that were to happen, and I believe that is not what you would want for me."

"I would not want that for anyone."

"I just hope that you understand how much it deeply pains me to put you through this again."

Miss Bradley followed the short, stocky man down a narrow hallway. They entered a small room where Emmett's deceased body was, covered with a white sheet on top of a brown wooden table. The funeral director reached over and snatched the sheet off the corpse. They stepped back a few feet to view the body at a distance, because of the terrible stench. Miss Bradley and Mr. Rayner stared with horror. The body was swollen almost twice its normal size. The neck had been ripped raw. The beating and three days in the river had turned the face and head into a monstrous mess of stinking flesh. The right eye was lying midway on Emmett's cheek. His tongue was choked out. His nose had been broken, like somebody took a meat chopper and hacked his nose in several places. There was a large bullet hole on the right side of Emmett's head. Miss Bradley and Mr. Rayner could look through the hole and see daylight on the other side.

Mr. Rayner hung his head down slowly, closing his eyes. "Is this your son, Miss Bradley?" he said sadly.

The heartbroken mother could not stop looking at her boy. It took a few seconds before she could even speak. "Yes it is," she said with plenty of sadness in her voice. "*This sickening sight done to a human being that was created by God is my son.*"

Mr. Rayner shook his head with disgust, while glaring at Emmett's corpse. "*Only someone possessed by the devil himself could of done something this horrific.*"

"*This is a terrible nightmare that I wish I was never a part of,*" Miss Bradley said with a touch of anger.

Mr. Rayner just glared at the pretty-faced woman in amazement. "*How on earth are you able to deal with this? You seem to be so remarkably poised and clear-headed about all of this.*"

Miss Bradley answered back, "*After I was told that Bobo had been murdered, I laid in my bedroom crying my eyes out over my son's death, until I heard a divine voice say to me, 'Not to worry. I lost my only son, too,' and at that very moment, I just knew right then and there that he was in a much better place.*"

"*So that is how you're able to stay so strong.*"

"*Thank you for those very kind words, but I must be leaving now.*"

"*Yes, of course. Well, you try and have a good evening, Miss Bradley, and may God bless you,*" he said, shaking her hand.

"*May God bless us all,*" Miss Bradley responded strongly.

Inside the courtroom, the tall attorney is standing in front of Miss Bradley. "That was quite a conversation that you and this funeral director had. But can you tell the court how you feel right now?"

"I am alone now. I have my mother and father, my relatives and friends, but still I am alone with my heart buried in a pine box underneath grass. I left my job because I have not yet become adjusted to being without my baby."

The district attorney looks at Miss Bradley. A smile appears across his face. "Thank you, Miss Bradley, for coming up here today. I do realize that being here in front of all these strangers could not have been an easy task for you at all. You are a very courageous woman. There will be no further questions."

"You may step down," Judge Swango says with half a smile.

Emmett's mother rises up from her chair and sits back down. "May I please say one last thing before I step down?"

"Go ahead," Judge Swango replies, with a serious look on his face.

"Just months ago I had a nice apartment in Chicago. I had a good job, but most importantly I had a loving son. When something awful used to happen to Negroes down here or anywhere in the South, I used to say that's their business, not mine. Now I know how very wrong that I was about that. The murder of my son has taught me that whatever happens to any of us in this country had better be the business of us all!"

Many whites in the courtroom are surprised to see this composed, articulate Negro woman in such a hostile environment. On her walk to the back of the courtroom, to the Negro press table, she notices angry faces staring at her from every direction. Miss Bradley sits down slowly in her seat.

The district attorney turns to the Judge. "Your Honor," he shouts across the courtroom, "I would like to call on the defendant, Roy Bryant, up to the witness stand."

Bryant walks boldly up to the stand with a cigar hanging from the corner of his mouth. He's wearing a white, short-sleeved shirt, tan slacks, and black lace-up shoes.

"Do you swear to tell the truth and nothing but the truth, so help you God?" the bailiff asks.

Bryant puts his left hand up in the air and his right hand on the Bible. "Yeah I do," he replies in an uncaring tone.

"Thank you, Mr. Bryant. You may be seated. Now sir," the attorney rushes up to the defendant with fire in his eyes, "are you aware that there is a lot of national attention from the newspapers indicating that all decent white people are outraged at you and Milam for being accused of this hateful and shameful crime on a fourteen-year-old boy!"

The bushy-eyebrowed redneck slowly lights his cigar and blows smoke in the attorney's face. "I don't know nothing about that," he exclaims with a devilish grin.

"I believe that you do," the attorney says, coughing from the thick smoke while fanning it away from his face.

"Tell the court what you and Milam really did to Emmett after taking him from his uncle's cabin."

"We only wanted to scare the boy, but when he refused to repent or beg for mercy, we had no choice but to teach him a lesson. But we didn't kill 'em!"

"And you expect this court and jury to believe that you and Milam did not kill this young boy?"

"I'm no bully. I never hurt a Nigra when they are in their place. But we had to put this Till boy in his place, especially after making a pass at my wife, and I know that any decent hard-working proud white man that is here today can understand that!"

The district attorney says in a fast and forceful voice, "And by putting him in his place was the reason why you and Milam drove him to the Tallahatchie River and ordered him to strip his clothes off at gunpoint, then you two beat on him when he refused to beg for his life, then you made him carry a seventy-five-pound cotton gin fan from the back of the truck, and then Milam shot him on the side of his head and murdered him?"

Bryant just smirks and calmly says, "You have some imagination on ya, don't ya'll."

The attorney turns to the Judge. "Your Honor, I would like to present to the jury the seventy-five-pound fan that was found tied with barbed wire around Emmett Till's neck when his body was pulled out of the river."

"Go ahead, counsel," the Judges nods.

The irritated lawyer motions for two deputies, who were holding onto the fan, to come forward. After they struggle to bring the large fan up to the witness stand, they place it on a table standing in front of the jury. The fan looked brown and rusty.

"Thank you," the attorney says to the deputies. They walk back to the front of the courtroom. The attorney turns towards Bryant. "Do you recognize this gin fan?"

"Nope."

"Why don't you take a good, long look at it," the attorney snaps, "because this is the fan that you and your half-brother used to dump Emmett's body with into the Tallahatchie River, but you two thought that this seventy-five-pound fan would keep his body from floating up. But as we all know, that plan sure backfired."

"Never seen that thang in my life!"

"Sure you haven't, just like you and Milam didn't murder little Emmett Till."

"That is enough," Judge Swango interrupts.

"Yes, your Honor." The attorney frowns, then he looks the accused killer directly in his big blue eyes. "Can you tell the court if you feel any kind of remorse about what happened to Emmett Till?"

"Remorse about what?" he says with an angry scowl.

"About murdering Emmett Till, Miss Bradley's only son, that's what!" he shouts at the top of his lungs.

The Judge gets red in the face. "I will advise you only one more time, Mr. Chatham, to knock it off. I want you to stop implying that Mr.

Bryant and Mr. Milam are murderous until it has been proven in this courtroom. Do I make myself clear this time, counsel?!"

"Yes, your Honor." The attorney turns back to the defendant. "What did you and Milam do to Emmett?"

Bryant gives a false smile. "Like I told ya'll, all we done is put a good old-fashioned scare in the boy, that's all."

"You do not know that there was an eyewitness who reported seeing you and Milam and two Negroes all inside a green pickup truck with Emmett at a remote shed by the Tallahatchie River, where his dead body was found only days later?"

"Don't know what you talking about. Why don't you ask this so-called witness of yours to come up here and tell us what he done saw."

"You know good and well that's not going to happen. And you know why it's not going to happen. He was too afraid to testify because of all the death threats that he had received if he did testify up here today!"

CHAPTER 5

"You people up North think we treat our Nigras so bad don't ya." Bryant says. "I have been reading the newspaper and all the magazine articles how folks all over the world is saying about us in Mississippi, every since that boy came down here and stir up all this trouble. We do treat our Nigras real good up here ya know!"

The district attorney nods his head sadly. "Can you explain that ridiculous comment?"

"It ain't ridiculous! The owner of this station in Natchez has a brother here. He sends a Nigra boy who works in Natchez station to come here nearly 200 miles to do work. Now doesn't that sound like we are loyal to a good Nigra down here, if they behave right?"

The attorney nods his head once again. "If you truly believe any of that nonsense that just came out of your mouth, there is really no real hope of you becoming a decent human being."

Judge Swango slams down his gavel on his desk with such a powerful force, he chips the side of his desk. His eyes bulge out, and his mouth starts to open. "You are really skating on thin ice in my court. Keep skating and that ice is going to break real soon!"

The attorney shrugs his shoulders. "Yes, your Honor."

"I will not have you insulting Mr. Bryant. You are here to only question the defendant. Anything more than that is crossing the line. Now go on with your questioning and watch yourself."

"Yes, your Honor." He pauses for a brief moment. "Bryant, did you and Milam take Emmett to the Tallahatchie River?"

"Yes we did, but we only just slapped him around, but we didn't kill 'em!"

"Yeah, there is no harm in two grown men slapping around a fourteen-year-old kid now, is there Bryant!"

"We can't let some Nigra boy from up North get away with coming on to a white woman. That would of sent a real bad message to all of the Nigra men in Mississippi. That it's okay to say or do anything to our white women!"

"Okay, Bryant," the attorney says quickly, "I just want you to tell the people in this courtroom exactly what really happened that morning after you and Milam abducted Emmett at gunpoint."

"Like I been saying, we just wanted to scare 'em, you know, put some fear in the boy, so we took 'em to the shed by the river to give him a good whumping and that's all!"

Bryant continues to explain to everyone inside of the courthouse his version of what he and Milam did to Emmett behind that shed by the river on Sunday morning, August 28. "We had the boy up against the shed by the river. His face and T-shirt was covered in blood. Milam was pistol-whipping him, while I was shining a flashlight in his face."

"Boy!" Bryant shouted. "Do you think that you can come down here and say anything that you want to a white woman and get away with it? Well, do ya?!"

"I was just joking around," Emmett said innocently.

Bryant cocked his right arm back as far as it could go and struck Emmett with the flashlight with a hard blow, knocking the Chicago boy to his knees. Emmett grabbed the side of his face. Blood streamed down his forehead. "What are you hitting me for, Mister?" The boy frowned.

"Because that pretty little white woman that you made sexual advancements to was my wife, nigger!"

Emmett stammered, "That w-was—your wife?!"

Milam quickly interrupted. "Look, you coon, we are very serious about how Nigra men act towards our white women down here in Mississippi!"

Bryant was hungry to hurt the young boy some more. "We gonna beat you so bad, the next time you ever lay your eyes on another white woman again, you gonna be pissing in your pants."

Milam pressed his .45 pistol hard on the side of Emmett's head. "Okay, coon, I want to hear you beg for your miserable life. Go on, beg, you stinking nigger!"

"No," Emmett said sternly.

Milam scratched the back of his head. "No?"

The two white men were in complete shock. Their jaws almost hit the ground. They became silent for a few seconds, looked at each other, and burst out laughing.

"This nigger is crazy!" Bryant said in disbelief.

"I got to admit," Milam confessed, "this boy got some pair of balls on him. All my years that I been dealing with this jigaboos, I never had any of them to ever tell me 'no' to my face, especially with a gun pointed at them. I never seen no shit like this before in all my days of living."

"Maybe this one is just too crazy to realize that you about to put a bullet in his brain," Bryant said.

"Oh, I think he's gonna realize that in a couple of seconds," Milam frowned up his face, pulling the trigger back on his .45.

Bryant yelled at Emmett, "We want to hear you beg, boy. Now start begging or die!"

"Why should I?" Emmett boldly blurted out. "You just going to kill me anyway."

Milam blind-sided the boy, smacking him with the butt of the gun on his jaw, knocking three of Emmett's front teeth clean out of his mouth. His back slammed up against the shed. He fell and rolled to the ground. A black-and-white photograph of a white teenage girl fell out of his pocket. She had long blonde hair, a cute face, and deep, big, blue eyes.

Bryant bent down on one knee and picked it up. He stood up completely still while he just gawked at the picture in horror, his mouth wide open. "I don't believe this!" he said in a state of shock. "J. W., get over here and take a look at what fell out of this boy's pocket."

Milam walked over to Bryant, who handed the broad-shouldered man the picture. He took one look at it and gave the photo back to Bryant without saying one word. He approached Emmett with fire in his eyes, grabbed him by his throat with one hand, and lifted the boy off his feet into the air. He looked up at him, as blood poured from Emmett's mouth. "What in the hell are you doing carrying a picture of a white gal in your pocket for? Answer me!" Milam hollered.

As Milam unwrapped his large hand from around Emmett's neck and dropped him onto the ground, the boy spurted, "She is my friend." Emmett rubbed his throat.

"What do you mean, she your friend?"

"She is my girlfriend."

"You had relations with her, boy?!" Milam shouted.

"Yeah, I did."

"Why you filthy nigger!" Bryant screamed. He began beating on

Emmett all over his body with the flashlight so hard that it was breaking apart.

Milam rushed up to Bryant and pulled him away from the youth. "Roy, stop it! We can't kill 'em. We will regret it for the rest of our lives. Remember that we both agreed that there be no killing, that we just was gonna teach him a good lesson."

"Yeah, I know," Bryant admitted, "but we had no idea that he was gonna talk back to us like this. And besides, he has a picture of some white gal that he had relations with."

"I know, I know, but killing 'em just ain't worth it. We just can't afford to go to prison over killing some coon. Come on, let's get out of here."

"I ain't scared of you white bastards," Emmett said through his swollen lips.

"What did you say, boy!" Milam asked with hot rage.

"I ain't scared of you white bastards," he repeated.

Milam ran up to Emmett with anger in his eyes, fists clenched tight, ready to strike.

Bryant jumped in between the hair-triggered white Southerner and Emmett. He placed both hands on Milam's large chest. "Don't do it, just let it go," Bryant pleaded. "Don't let this Nigra provoke you like that, J. W."

"If you think I'm afraid, I'm not. I stood up to white men that was a lot tougher than you two," Emmett roared.

"Shut your mouth up, nigger!" Milam raised his voice.

"What kind of courage does it really take for two grown men to pick on a kid anyway?" Emmett asked.

"Shut your big fat mouth up, coon," Milam said in a louder tone, with disgust on his face.

"You two ain't nothing but a couple of cowards, that's what you are!"

Milam turned to Bryant, full of frustration. "I can't take no more of this back talk from this coon!"

"Calm down, J. W. Don't lose your temper. Don't forget that you were the one who said to me, 'Don't kill 'em because we can't afford to go to prison over killing some coon,' remember that?"

"I know what I said, but I swear 'fore God if this boy say one more thang, I'm gonna beat his brains out, then I'm gonna shoot him dead!"

"No!" Bryant responded. "Let's just take this boy back to the truck and drop him off in town."

"But do you think this boy has learn his lesson about sassing white women?" Bryant turned to face Emmett. "Well, have ya, boy?!"

"You going to let me live?"

"If you keep your mouth shut, we will," Milam stated.

"I just wanna go back to my uncle's cabin."

"Don't push your luck, boy. We dropping you in town. You can walk back to your uncle's cabin, far as I am concerned," Milam said with a smug expression.

"You should be glad that we're gonna let you live," Bryant added. He started rubbing his right arm and grimaced.

"What's wrong with you?"

"I must of popped a joint out when I was beating on this nigger with this flashlight."

Milam laughed, "You know those coons got heads harder than a rock!"

"Why do ya hate me so much? You don't even know nothing about me," Emmett asked.

"You sass my wife!" Bryant answered with anger.

"And you beat me for that?"

"A lot of Nigras would have been killed for what you done."

"That is so stupid!"

"It ain't stupid. Once a Nigra thinks he can say anything to a white woman, there ain't no telling what he'll do next!"

Emmett took a long look at Milam and Bryant, made a quick observation, and shook his head. "It sound like you two are afraid of the black man to me!"

"Afraid!" Milam chuckled. "You must be kidding. There nothing to be afraid of. Ya'll is dumb, weak, lazy, and you all are afraid of your own shadows."

"If we are all those things, then why do you hate us so much? We should not be no threat to you!"

CHAPTER 6

"You are talking way too much!"

"I just want to know why the color of my skin scares you so much."

Anger pinched the corner of Milam's mouth. "That is enough!"

Emmett completely ignored the words of the big white man and still continued to express himself. "You know, back in Chicago, I knew this bully in school who always picked on people. One day I ask him, why did he do it. He said because it made him feel good about himself, because deep down inside he didn't like who he was."

"Are you trying to say that the white man don't like who he is?!" Milam shouted, drenched with sweat from the hot heat.

"I'm saying that you two remind me of that bully. I knew in school. You only pick on folks that can't fight back, because you two is really just cowards!"

Milam looked like a lion about to rip into some fresh meat. "Do you hear this uppity Northern nigger!" he screamed like a crazy man. "We can't let him live now, no way!" He walked up to Emmett.

Bryant jumped in front of him again. "We can't kill 'em, J. W. We just can't do it."

Milam had a defeated look on his face. He stuck his pistol in

Emmett's back. "Let's go, and you better not say another goddamn thang. And I mean that!"

They all three walked back to the truck. Emmett climbed in the back. Bryant and Milam went up front, and they drove off.

"Wow, what a story," the district attorney says in a sarcastic tone. "Your Honor, I had just enough that I can stomach from this witness. No further questions."

"You may be seated," Judge Swango says to Bryant.

"So I'm finished?"

"If justice triumphs in this courtroom today, I certainly hope so!" the attorney says with a sharp tone.

Bryant gives the attorney a long, hard, hateful glare. He slowly stands up and walks back to his table and sits down next to his wife.

The district attorney steps down from the bench, while the defense attorney, Mr. Carleton, walks back up to the bench. "The State calls on Mrs. Bryant to the witness stand!" he shouts.

A very pretty white woman, with huge blue eyes and creamy skin, stands up from the table. She pats Bryant on the shoulder, steps around him, and walks up to the witness stand.

"Raise your right hand up," the bailiff says politely, "and place your left hand on the Bible, Mrs. Bryant."

She does exactly what the bailiff asks of her.

"Do you swear to tell the truth and nothing but the truth, so help you God?"

"Yes I do."

"Take your seat, Mrs. Bryant."

She sits down, wearing her tight-fitting skirt, in the witness chair. The front of her long, black hair has been combed loosely across her head. The hair falls over her eyes, and she has to shake it back.

"My, that is a pretty skirt that you are wearing, Mrs. Bryant," the bailiff says with a smile.

"Why thank you, Fred!" she replies, smiling, showing off her pearly white teeth.

"Could you state your full name?" the defense attorney asks her in a firm tone.

"Carolyn Bryant," she answers in a soft voice, crossing her smooth, shining legs.

"When were you married, Mrs. Bryant?"

"April 25, 1951."

"Did your husband serve in the Armed Forces?"

"Yes he did."

"How long was Bryant in service?"

"Three years."

"Mrs. Bryant, is it true that you were voted most beautiful girl at two of your former high schools, Indianola and Leland?"

"Yes."

"On Wednesday evening, August 24, who was in the store with you?"

"I was by myself."

"Did anything unusual occur that day?"

"Yes."

"Tell the court what happened on that day."

Mrs. Bryant begins to tell her side of the story on what happened. This was the kind of show many of the whites in the audience had come for. They lean forward in their seats to better hear all the juicy details of the alleged assault that had taken place on that hot summer day. She starts at the very beginning. All the reporters take down every word of Carolyn Bryant's testimony.

"Around 7:30 p.m., I see four Negro boys and an old Negro man standing outside. I seen them from out of the store window. I could see what they were doing, but I couldn't hear what they were saying."

Outside, next to a little grocery store, Curtis was playing checkers with an old man. Emmett and his cousin, Maurice, and another boy were watching them. Emmett had a set of perfect white teeth. He wore a brown straw hat. He had funny-looking light colored eyes that the girls back in Chicago found very attractive. His clothes set him apart from the rest of the Negroes: black leather dress shoes, pants, and a white shirt. He looked nothing like a country boy.

"H-hey, you cats w-want to see something?" Emmett stammered.

"See what?" one of the local boys answered. He was a very light-skinned Negro kid with red hair and brown freckles dotted across his big cheeks.

"A picture of a white girl," Emmett answered back.

"You must be out of your damn mind!"

Maurice, Emmett's cousin, who had round, wide eyes, spoke in a heavy voice. "This fool ain't got no picture of no white gal."

The old man, who appeared to be in his late eighties, just nodded sadly. He slowly said, "Well, if he does, he better keep it right in his damn pocket. You can get strung up by your neck for carrying around a picture of some white gal on you. Don't ya know that, boy?"

Curtis turned around towards Emmett and looked directly at him. "Don't worry, mister, he just lying anyway," he implied. "Bobo just trying to bring himself some attention. He do not have a picture of a white girl nowhere in his pockets."

"I bet I do."

"I bet you don't," Maurice declared.

"How much you wanna bet?"

"Ten cent."

"It's a bet!"

Emmett pulled out a photograph and passed it around to the group of boys.

"Holy shit, it's a picture of a white gal alright!" Maurice shouted in amazement.

"It sho' is," the boy with the freckles said.

Curtis was shocked from the thought that his cousin could be carrying a picture of some white girl in his pocket. "Let me see this." He snatched the photo and held it in his hand. Beaming down at it, he was hypnotized by what his eyes were showing him. "Where did you get this?!" he asked with concern.

Maurice spoke before Emmett could even answer Curtis's question. "He found it on some sidewalk," he said jokingly. Maurice and the freckled-face boy burst out laughing.

"It ain't funny," the old man warned them. "If white folk catch him with that in his pocket, they gonna kick the living hell out of him."

"I ain't scare of no white folk," Emmett announced proudly.

"You better be. Maybe where you come from you can get away with some things with white folk. But down here, white folk is crazy. They will take a colored person's life as quick as they would swat a fly off the wall!"

"Don't lessen to this old man. He just like to hear hisself talk," the red-haired boy said.

"Hey, Bobo," Maurice smiled. "There is a pretty looking white woman working in that store. I dare you to ask her for a date."

"You don't think I won't?"

"No way, you ain't got the guts to do something that brave."

"You mean something that stupid. Don't you do it, boy!" the elderly man advised.

"I ain't scare of nothing. I'm going in there and I'm going to say something to her right now," Emmett said, stomping his foot.

"If you try and ask that white woman for a date, you won't live long

enough to brag about it." Everyone around Money, Mississippi, knew that Carolyn Bryant had won a couple of local beauty contests, making her one of the best-known young white women in the area. The local boys and the old man knew the risk of talking to her or even looking her in the eyes. Asking her on a date would be unimaginable.

"You are not going inside that store," Curtis said to Emmett. "And you going to get rid of that picture, too."

"You may be my older cousin, but that don't mean you can boss me around."

"I just don't want you to do anything silly, that's all."

"Relax. I'm going inside that store just to buy some candy."

"Are you sure that's all you're going to do?"

"Yeah, I am sure. And I'm going to buy you some candy, too."

"What about the picture?"

"I'm not getting rid of a picture of my girlfriend."

"Girlfriend! I think o' Bobo may have fell on top of his head way too many times when he was a baby!" Maurice smirked.

The local boys laughed out loud at the Chicago boy, really giving him a hard time.

Emmett stuttered, "I- I—don't like it w-when pe-people laugh at me!"

Maurice looked Emmett up and down. "You should be used to it by now."

Emmett looked Maurice in his eyes. "Don't you owe me ten cent?"

"Yeah."

"Give me my money, then!"

His cousin with the heavy voice reached down in his pocket and gave the Northern kid his dime. Emmett began walking towards the grocery store, very upset.

"Hey Bobo, don't be mad," the red-haired kid yelled at Emmett. "Maybe *you should just ask that white woman in the sto' to be your gal friend. Then that way you'll have two white gal friends instead of just one!"*

The slide remark caused the Southern boys to laugh at the Chicago boy once again. He turned around and walked back to the group. "You color folk down here is just way too scary for me."

The old man responded very quickly, "You live down here long enough, boy, and you'll know just why."

"I'm going in that store, and I'm going to show you cats that I'm not scare of nothing, and I bet you won't laugh at me then."

"Wait a minute, Bobo," Curtis said with worry. "You just said that you were buying some candy."

"I change my mind!" he said with a straight face.

"Look, there is no need for you to start showing out. You do not have anything to prove to anyone here."

Emmett started walking back towards the store. Curtis began to panic. "Bobo! Bobo! Come back here!"

"Let him go, Curtis," Maurice said. "That fool is just gonna buy some candy, and that's all he's gonna do."

CHAPTER 7

"Yeah, with your money," the freckled-face boy pronounced.

"Well, he still ain't crazy enough to talk to no white woman," Maurice said.

"You just don't know Bobo." Curtis said, his face filled with plenty of concern.

The old man nodded his head again. "I have a bad feeling about this, a real bad feeling."

Inside of the store, Mrs. Bryant was standing by the cash register. Emmett came into the store and walked up to the candy case. Then Mrs. Bryant walked up behind the candy case. "What do you want?" She frowned.

"I want a couple of those Tootsie Rolls over there!" Emmett demanded.

Mrs. Bryant's eyes got wide and mean-looking. "I don't know where you from, but down here you address me as Mrs. or ma'am!"

"Sorry, ma'am, can I have a couple Tootsie Rolls over there?" he asked gently.

"That's better!" she said in a stern voice.

Mrs. Bryant grabbed the candy out of the case and handed it to Emmett. He rubbed his hand against hers. Mrs. Bryant's face became redder than a shining apple. "You just touched me, and you did it on purpose, too."

"No I didn't," he harshly disagreed.

"I think it be best if you left my store, and I mean right now!!"

Curtis barged inside the store with a spooked look. He just knew in his gut that Emmett had done something wrong. Judging by the facial expression on the young white woman, things were about to get heated. "What did you do, Bobo?" he pleaded.

"You better get him out of here, and I mean real fast, 'fore something bad happens to this boy," she snapped.

Without any hesitation, Curtis snatched his fearless cousin by his arm, pulling him towards the door. "Come on, Bobo, let's get out of here!" he said in a very shaken voice.

When Emmett got closer to the door, he stopped, smiled, and looked directly at the former beauty winner. "Bye-bye, baby." He whistled at her in the two-note wolf whistle.

Curtis immediately pushed Emmett in the back with his two hands, out of the door. As the two boys approached the old man and the two boys, the old man couldn't keep his eyes off of Curtis.

"I can tell by the look on your face that something really bad happen in that sto'."

Curtis was fidgeting out of control. "Bobo just whistle at that white woman back inside that store and said, 'Bye-bye, baby' to her when we was leaving out."

"Oh, you then done it now, boy!" the old man shouted out loud. "You then really done it now!"

Mrs. Bryant came out of the store looking meaner than a swarm of angry hornets. She headed towards a 1951 blue and white Buick.

"What she going to-to—d-do?" Emmett stuttered.

"Oh, you getting scare now, huh, boy, and you should be. That Mrs. Bryant has a mean o' brother-in-law." The old man continued, "He owns *a .45 that he loan her. She keeps it in her car, and she gonna blow your balls off with it."*

After those harsh words were spoken, Curtis's racing heart started to skip several beats. "How do you know that she has a gun, mister?"

"Because I come here every morning to play checkers, and every morning I see her take that pistol out of her purse and she puts it inside of her glove compartment."

"Why would she go get a gun? I was just playing around."

"Boy, you can't play around with white folk down here." The old Negro man turned to Curtis and advised him, "You better get him out of here, before she shoot this boy dead, and you can't say that I didn't try to warn ya!"

"Come on, Bobo, Maurice. Let's go," Curtis shouted nervously. "We really need to get out of here."

Curtis, Bobo, and Maurice ran and jumped inside a 1941 gray Ford automobile. Curtis got behind the steering wheel and took off like they were fleeing from the bowels of hell.

When Mrs. Bryant finishes giving her testimony, the courtroom turns silent, the air hot with hatred. She keeps shifting in the witness stand, not sure where to put her hands, not sure where to look. When she makes eye contact with her husband, he nods, and she stops fidgeting.

"Mrs. Bryant, can you tell me how did this Nigra whistle at you?"

Mrs. Bryant looks up at Mr. Carleton as if she doesn't understand the question.

He picks up on that right away. "Did he whistle like this?" The defense attorney puckers his lips and makes the noise known nationally and universally as a wolf whistle.

She thinks for a while. "Yes!" she blurts out. "That is how the Negro man whistle at me."

"How tall was this Nigra man that came into your store?"

The district attorney stands up quickly from his seat. "I object, your Honor!"

"On what grounds?" the Judge asks.

"On the grounds that Mrs. Bryant and Mr. Carleton is referring to Emmett as being a man when he was only just a fourteen-year-old child."

"Overruled."

"But your Honor, it is ridiculous for anyone to call a fourteen-year-old male child a grown man."

"I said objection is overruled, and that is just what I meant, Mr. Chatham!"

"Yes sir, your Honor," he says, gritting his teeth.

"Now Mr. Carleton, go on with your witness," the Judge says.

The defense attorney glances over his shoulder at Mr. Chatham and grins at him. "Now, how tall was this Nigra man, Mrs. Bryant? About six feet tall?"

"That is absurd. Emmett Till was only five-six!!" Mr. Chatham shouts.

The Judge stands up from his desk with great speed, bangs his gavel several times on top of his desk. "One more outburst and I will have the bailiff remove you out of my courtroom. Do we have an understanding, Mr. Chatham?"

"Yes, your Honor."

"Continue on, Mr. Carleton!" Judge Swago says, sitting back down in his chair.

"Mrs. Bryant, how much would you estimate that the Negro man weighed, two hundred pounds maybe?"

"He was about two hundred and fifty pounds."

The district attorney puts his hand quickly over his mouth and leans back in his chair.

"Did he have a speech impediment?" the defense attorney asks.

"Yes," Mrs. Bryant replies.

"How did you feel when this ugly incident happened to you?"

"I was so scared, and he didn't look fourteen to me. He look like a grown man," Mrs. Bryant says in a hard tone.

"Do you know most of the Nigras around Money?"

"Yes I do. Money is a small rural community of Leflore County, deep in the cotton-rich Mississippi delta."

"Was this Nigra from there?"

"No."

"Did he talk with a Southern or Northern brogue?"

"Northern."

"Was Mr. Bryant out of town that day?"

"Yes, he had gone to Louisiana and Brownsville, Texas, to take a load of shrimp over there."

"So you had no white men around to protect you?"

"Mr. Milam, my brother-in-law, was visiting and would help out in the store when I needed it. He stayed up here so I wouldn't be by myself. But he wasn't in the store that day."

"Thank you, Mrs. Bryant. There be no further questions, your Honor."

The Judge looks at Mrs. Bryant. "You may take your seat now."

She steps down from the witness stand and sits back down in her chair at the table next to her husband and children. The defense attorney, Mr. Carleton, returns to his seat, and the district attorney, Mr. Chatham, steps back up to the witness stand.

"The State calls on J. W. Milam up to the stand."

A tall, strapping white man with a twisted mouth walks up to the witness stand holding a cigar in his hand. As he approaches the bench, the courtroom becomes completely silent. The bailiff is there to greet the intimidating figure.

"Do you swear to tell the truth and nothing but the truth, so help you God?"

"You damn right I do," he says, placing his right hand on the Bible and raising up his left hand.

"Have a seat, J. W.," the bailiff says with plenty of respect.

Milam sits down with an uncaring look on his face.

"How's the wife and kids holding up, J. W.?"

"They doing the best that they can."

"We still on for golf next week?"

Just looking at Milam's cold demeanor, no one would be able to guess that he is on trial for murder. "I wouldn't miss it," he replies back to the bailiff.

"Are you done, Milam?" Mr. Chatham shouts in a very stern tone.

"What's the matter?" he scowls. "You got something against playing golf?"

"No, I have a problem with anyone coming into a courtroom and treating it like a social event."

"I'm just being neighborly," he says, giving a fake smile.

"Let's just get right down to it, Milam. Did you and your half-brother, Roy Bryant, kill Emmett Till on August 28, Sunday morning?"

"No, did you?" he says with a big smile.

The rude remark causes the disrespectful white audience to break into laughter.

"There is nothing at all that is funny about murder, Milam."

"Let me tell ya one thang, Mister District Attorney. My daddy use to always tell me when I was only knee high, a real good nigger is a dead nigger."

Mr. Chatham can't believe what he is hearing. He turns to the Judge with a disappointed look on his face. "Your Honor, are you really going to allow this defendant to speak like this in a court of law?"

"You just focus on questioning Mr. Milam and let me handle what goes on in my courtroom!"

"But your Honor, I—"

Judge Swango interrupts him. "But nothing, Mr. Chatham. Just proceed."

Mr. Chatham takes a deep breath and turns to face Milam. "Did you and Bryant take Emmett from Mr. Wright's cabin?"

"We did, but all we done is give the little jigaboo a good whumping, and then we let him go, just like Roy told ya."

"And you expect me to believe that!"

"I don't give a damn what you believe. It's the truth," Milam says with a frown.

The attorney points his finger at the insensitive Southerner. "You are a liar, Milam!" he shouts at him. "You and Bryant killed a fourteen-year-old boy and don't even have the guts to even admit it."

The defense attorney, Mr. Carleton, jumps up from his chair. "Objection, your Honor!"

"On what grounds?" Judge Swango asks.

"I think that Mr. Chatham is way out of line here in the manner that he is speaking to Mr. Milam."

"Mr. Chatham chuckles. "You have got to be kidding. This man has done nothing but disrespect this courtroom with all his vulgar comments since the time he stepped up to this witness stand."

Judge Swango thinks a moment, then says with a somber glare, "Be careful on how you speak to the defendant."

"How I'm speaking to the defendant? How about the way the defendant is speaking, with all his racist rhetoric!"

"I'm warning you, counsel!!"

"This can't be real," he says in disbelief.

"You are just seconds away from me kicking you out of my courtroom, do you understand me?"

CHAPTER 8

"Yes, your Honor."

Judge Swango's voice suddenly turns mean. "You're really pushing it, counsel."

"Sorry, your Honor," the attorney says with hesitation in his voice, then, turning towards Milam, looking him straight into his narrow eyes. "How do you feel about a Negro man dating a white woman?" he says quickly, waiting for an answer.

"How do I feel," Milam says with disgust. "It makes my skin crawl just thinking about it. God don't want our women mixing with no monkeys."

The white audience snickers loudly.

"What would you do if you saw a Negro man just looking at a white woman for too long?"

"I would beat his brains out, that's what I would do."

"Even kill him?"

Milam's eyes became wide and weird looking. "Look, this whole thing is nothing but a joke anyway. Do you think anyone in Mississippi is gonna go to jail for killing a damn jigaboo, and even if we did kill this little monkey, we ain't gonna do no time for it."

"Is this your own dumb little way of admitting to killing Emmett Till?"

"No, but I tell you what is dumb. That I am sitting here on this witness stand being excuse of killing some black monkey that no real white man gives a rat's ass about!"

Mr. Chatham nods his head. "You are some piece of work, you know that, Milam."

"Yeah, I know." He gives an ugly grin. "When God made me, He really broke the mold, huh?"

"It's more like the devil made you than God."

"Let's be honest about this whole thang. Every decent white person in Mississippi believes that this little monkey got exactly what he deserved!"

"There are some people who do care about what did happen to Emmett Till, and it doesn't paint a very good picture to them that two grown men are being accused of taking the life of a minor because he just whistled at a white woman."

"Far as I am concerned, the whole country should think and believe like we do down here."

"Whistling at a white woman is not a crime, Milam."

"It is if you a jigaboo," he smiles.

"Are you a member of the K.K.K., Milam?"

"No, but I think your mama is," he blurts out.

All the whites in the courtroom once again burst into laughter. Judge Swango is on the crowd like a grizzly bear. He bangs his gavel on his desk. "We'll have none of that here—not today, not until this trial is over. You people who can't be respectful of the law might just leave now, because if I hear anything else, I will have the bailiff throw you out."

The room gets quiet right away. Mr. Chatham clears his voice before speaking back to Milam. "If what you say is so true, about nobody in

Mississippi caring about a white man killing a Negro, just fess up to it like a real white man. I'm pretty sure it will make you a local hero among all your redneck buddies."

The courtroom is still quiet. Milam stares long and very hard at the district attorney, down at his feet, then to the top of his head. "You ain't no real white man," he grumbles loudly. "You a Jew boy, ain't ya?"

"I am a human being. That is the least that I can say about you," he said in a calm voice.

"You're lucky that we're in a courtroom, boy!"

"You don't scare me, Milam—why don't you just tell the truth, so we can all go home, and just admit that you and Bryant murdered Emmett Till, a fourteen-year-old kid?!" he screams at the defendant. Then he quickly glances nervously over his shoulder at Judge Swango.

Milam's forehead wrinkles, "How many goddamn times do I have to tell you, we didn't murder no nigger!"

"How do you think it would make you look to all your Klan pals if they were to find out that you were too afraid to admit that you killed, as you would put it, some monkey? You're a big man in this town. I heard that everyone in Mississippi looks up to you. Do you think once the word gets out that big, tough Milam was too afraid to confess to killing a low-life nigger, that people in this town will ever look up to you any longer?"

Milam almost jumps out of his chair. He violently pounds his chest repeatedly. "I ain't afraid of nothing. I am a real white man!" he yells.

"Well, prove it then," Mr. Chatham grins. "Be a real white man and tell the truth. Like you just said, no one is going to indict no white man in Mississippi for killing no jigaboo, right? Now stop being such a coward and tell these people who are all here today the truth. Or maybe you can't do it, because you are just a snot-nose coward!"

Milam's eyes turn red as hot fire. Spit is flying out of his mouth.

"That is twice you have called me a coward. My daddy didn't raise no cowards. Okay, okay, we—"

Bryant stands up from the table and yells, "Don't do it, J.W. It's a trick!!"

The Judge raps his gavel five times on his desk. Bryant sits back down, and so does Milam.

"Order, order in my courtroom. Now," the Judge pauses and turns to Mr. Chatham, "proceed with this case."

"Did you murder Emmett Till, yes or no?!"

"Like I said, we didn't murder no goddamn nigger!!"

The district attorney starts wiping the sweat from the back of his neck with his handkerchief.

"Too hot for you, huh, boy? Well, we Mississippians are just used to all this heat down here. I hope all that sweating ain't gonna shrink up that cheap shirt and tie that you wearing," Milam smirks.

Mr. Chatham gives him an unpleasant look. "There will be no more further questions, your Honor. This defendant wouldn't know the truth if it bit him on his big fat bald head!"

Milam waves as he leaves the witness stand. "Bye-bye, Jew boy," he smiles.

The district attorney rolls his eyes and sits down at his table. The defense attorney, Mr. Carleton, steps up to the witness stand and announces, "The defense calls on Sheriff Strider."

Sheriff Strider appears from the back door in full uniform, sporting some dark shades and smacking his gum loudly. He is a heavy-set man with a round belly, who sweats all the time. He pushes through the crowd and makes it up slowly to the witness stand.

"Have a seat, Sheriff," the bailiff says.

He sits down in the witness chair. The defense attorney walks in front of him. "Sheriff Strider, did you have occasion on August 31, when the body was taken from the Tallahatchie River, to examine it down there?"

I did. I arrived about 9:15 A.M., and the body was in a boat and had not yet been placed on the river bank."

"Did you examine the body down there?"

"The best that I could."

"What was the condition of the body?"

"It was in mighty bad shape," he says, smacking his chewing gum. "The skin was slipping off the entire body. The skull was crushed. There was a penetration above the right ear, and there was three gashes on the head. I took a small stick about the size of a pencil and probed the hole above the right ear. I couldn't find any evidence of a bullet. The tongue extended from the mouth about three inches, and the left eyeball was out, just enough to call it out. Oh yeah," he adds, "and the boy's manhood had been chopped clean off!"

The white crowd quickly snickers.

"Was there an odor, Sheriff?" the defense attorney asks.

"Hell, yeah, it smell like roadkill that's been left in the sun for too long."

"Sheriff, you have lived near the Tallahatchie River for many years, so you must be familiar with temperature of the water at different seasons of the year and depth of the river generally."

"Yes I am."

"What would be the temperature during August, would you say?"

"I would say around seventy degrees."

"Have you ever taken a body out of the river that has been in there for three days?"

"Yes I have."

"Sheriff, what in your professional opinion, about how long this particular body had been in the river?"

He begins chewing his gum very loudly. "That body been in the water a good two weeks long before that Nigra got himself kidnapped. The corpse we pulled out of the Tallahatchie was no more that Till boy than I am a jackass!"

"Was the body taken from the Tallahatchie River recognizable?"

"The body was bloated beyond recognition, and I was unable to determine whether the body was a white man or Nigra. The body's only characteristic of being a Nigra was its kinky hair, but I seen lots of white men with kinky hair before."

"Sheriff Strider, what do you think about this murder?"

"No one actually seen this boy being murdered. I personally believe the body that was dredged up from the Tallahatchie River wasn't that Chicago boy at all. I think the NAACP had plotted the boy's killing. He probably somewhere in Chicago right now, as I speak."

"Was there a death certificate made out identifying the body as that of Emmett Till?"

"There was no death certificate issued, because I would not identify the body as that of Emmett Till. I went to the river with the boy's uncle, Mose Wright. I asked him, 'Was this the boy?'"

"And what did he say?"

"He said he didn't know for sure."

"Who found the body?"

"Some fourteen-year-old white kid fishing found the Nigra floating in the Tallahatchie River. The kid saw a pair of knees sticking out of the shallow water. He wasn't sure what the hell it was, so he contacted me."

"Is it true, Sheriff Strider, that you had received plenty of threats and hate mail when this Nigra boy came up missing?"

"I'm glad that you brought that up, because I just want to tell all those people sending me threatening letters, if I ever find out who you is, the same thing gonna happen to you that happen to that Chicago boy!"

The district attorney, Mr. Chatham, stands straight up from his chair with an irritated expression. "Objection!" he shouts.

Judge Swango leans back in his chair, crosses his arms, and gives Mr. Chatham a somber look. "On what grounds?"

"Your Honor, what exactly is the Sheriff trying to say here? He just said only a few moments ago in this very courtroom that Emmett may be somewhere in Chicago, that the body he pulled out of the river wasn't Emmett's body at all. Then he makes a statement like that? It sounds to me like Sheriff Strider needs to make up his mind about what he is really trying to say here."

Mr. Carleton interrupts in a hurry. "Your Honor, I'm pretty sure that the Sheriff just became a little excited, that's all," he explains in a nervous voice.

"Overruled. It has been a long, hot day," Judge Swango replies.

"That is no surprise," Mr. Chatham mumbles under his breath.

"What did you say, counsel?"

The district attorney sits back down at his table, like a little kid who has just gotten in trouble. "Nothing, your Honor."

"Proceed, Mr. Carleton," the Judge says, crossing his eyes at Mr. Chatham.

"Sheriff, have it been reported that thousands of Northern Nigras were on their way to Mississippi to tear down the jail to take Mr. Bryant and Mr. Milam?"

"If these Nigras think for one split second that they are coming down here to take over, we will have something for them, that's for sho'."

Mr. Carleton gives a short laugh. "Thank you very much, Sheriff Strider for your testimony. No further questions, your Honor."

"You may go back to your seat now, Sheriff," Judge Swango then adds.

He returns to his seat, still smacking on his gum.

Mr. Carleton shouts, "The defense calls Emmett Till's uncle up to the witness stand."

Two young Negro men help Mose Wright from the back of the Colored section. They have to push their way through the courtroom to get up to the witness stand. After escorting him, the two men return to their seats.

The bailiff stands in front of the elderly Negro. "Put your left hand on the Bible and raise your right hand."

The five-foot-three Mose raises his left hand.

"No, your right hand up, boy!" the bailiff scowls.

He raises his right hand and places his left hand on the Bible.

"Do you swear to tell the truth and nothing but the truth, so help you God?"

"Yas I does, suh." He sits down. The chair is almost too big for the small man, who is under the hateful glares of hundreds of very hostile spectators. He sits uncomfortably on its edge, waiting for his opportunity to testify. Mr. Carleton stares at the old man with a disgusting look on his face."

"State your full name, boy."

"Mose Wright, suh."

Mr. Carleton wipes the sweat from his face, then folds his arms and looks directly into Mose's eyes. "I want you to point out the two men in this courtroom that you believe without a shadow of a doubt killed your nephew."

Mose Wright straightens up and looks at Bryant and Milam at the defense table. Nobody moved, not even the children in the courtroom. Everybody holds their breaths, as if waiting for a bomb to go off. In silence, they wonder if Mose will risk his life to accuse two white men in open court. Excruciating tension fills the room.

Mose stands up, raises his arm, and points at the two defendants. "Thar they is!!"

The blood boils in hundreds of whites as they sit glaring in the courtroom at Mose. Even the defense attorney, Mr. Carleton, is shocked that he would do it. He had no idea that Mose would call his bluff. Everyone who has been holding their breath lets it out all at once and start talking. Someone shouts, "Lynch the nigger!"

It takes Judge Swango a lot of pounding and shouting to get things orderly again.

After everything calms down, Mr. Carleton does not hesitate to go right at Mose. "Isn't it a fact that the first time you ever laid eyes on Mr. Bryant and Mr. Milam was in the front page of a Mississippi newspaper? Isn't that true, boy?"

"No, that is not true, suh."

"You are not a very smart boy, are you? What do you have, a first-grade education, or maybe a second grade education—or maybe you don't have any education at all, boy!!"

"Objection!" Mr. Chatham jumps to his feet.

"On what grounds?" Judge Swango frowns.

"On the grounds that the defense attorney is badgering the witness about the level of his education, which has no relevance in this trial at all."

"But it does, your Honor," the defense attorney protests. "Why in the world should the jury believe the testimony of a man who probably can't read or write?"

"In all my years as a lawyer, that is one of the most absurd things that I have ever heard. Your Honor, whether Mr. Wright has any type of education does not take away the main fact that this witness has eyes and ears and that he knows exactly what he saw and heard. Having no education has nothing to do with Mr. Wright being capable of telling the people in this courtroom exactly what he knows about this case."

CHAPTER 9

Judge Swango takes his time before he responds. "Counsel has a pretty good argument this time. Mr. Carleton, this court does not care about the level of Wright's education. It is only interested in what he knows about this case."

Mr. Chatham looks at the Judge with disbelief. "Don't be so shocked, Mr. Chatham. I can be fair!"

"Proceed with the witness, Mr. Carleton."

"Yes, your Honor." The defense attorney frowns at Mr. Chatham, then turns to Mose. "When you first saw the body when it was pulled out of the river, did you know right away that it was the Nigra, well did ya, boy?!"

"Not right away."

"Not right away what!"

"I don't know what else that you want me to say."

"How about not right away, sir!"

"I can do that as soon as you can stop calling me 'boy.' Anyone with eyes can see that I am not a boy."

The whites listen, horrified. The courtroom becomes very silent. At any second it seems as if it is going to explode again.

Just then, a dark-complected Negro man, wearing a white T-shirt and a pair of ripped up blue jeans, walks through the back door. The Judge spots the nervous teenager right away. "You back there, who are you?" he shouts.

"My name is Willie Reed, son of a sharecropper. I seen the Chicago boy being killed at about 6 A.M. in the morning."

All of the whites in the courtroom shout and scream at Willie, calling him every racist name they can think of. Judge Swango pounds his gavel repeatedly to restore order in the courtroom. "If I have to pound this gavel one more time today, this trial will be dismissed until another day. I hope that I am making myself very clear to everyone in this courtroom!" He then points his finger towards Willie Reed. "Now you come up here, before you cause a riot in my courtroom."

The teenage boy begins approaching the witness stand. The Judge glances hard at Mose. "You can step down now. I think that you have said quite enough for one day!"

The small old man struggles to rise up from his chair. The Judge asks, "Could one of you Negroes back there come up here and help him back to his seat, so we can go on with this trial?" The same two Negro men who helped Mr. Wright before come and help him. Again, they have to push through the milling crowd of whites to make it to the back of the courtroom.

Willie Reed goes forward, up to the witness stand. Judge Swango looks at the defense attorney. "You may step down, now, Mr. Carleton, so the district attorney, Mr. Chatham, can cross-examine his so-called witness!"

The defense attorney slowly steps down, then the district attorney walks up to the bench. As the very frightened Willie Reed walks up to the witness stand, it looks like people in the courtroom are going to jump out of their seats and knock him down. Glares of hate and pure meanness follow him all the way up to the stand.

The bailiff swears in the young Negro, and he sits down.

"Willie," Mr. Chatham starts with a big smile, "I am very glad that you decided to change your mind about testifying today, because, as you may well know, things have got to change down here in Mississippi. Now, can you tell the court what you saw on Sunday morning, August the twenty-eighth?"

"Well, around six in the morning, I was on my way to buy meat for breakfast. That's when I seen the Chicago boy sitting in the back of a green pickup truck with two Negroes. Mr. Bryant and Mr. Milam were inside of the truck. They all went to a remote shed on the old plantation."

"What happened at that shed on August 28?"

The Negro boy looks around at the mean white faces inside the courtroom. He doesn't take his eyes off of them while he gives his testimony. "As I said, it was about six o'clock in the morning. I was hiding behind a wooden fence by the Tallahatchie River and watched Mr. Bryant and Mr. Milam getting out of a green pickup truck. Levy Collins and Willie Loggins was taking the Chicago boy down from the back of the truck."

"Hurry it up!" Milam shouted. "And bring that boy down here!"

The two Negro men brought Emmett to them. Bryant had blood splattered down the front of his white T-shirt. "Boy, what in the hell makes you think that you can go around saying whatever you like to a white woman?!"

Emmett didn't say anything.

Milam, with fire in his eyes, pulled out his pistol from his black leather holster. He pressed it up against Emmett's forehead. "Answer him, nigger!!" he screamed in his face.

"I didn't mean anything by it."

"If I were you, I would be begging for my life right about now."

"I'm not begging for nothin'," the Northern boy said boldly.

Milam shook his head in frustration. "You stupid coon, don't you know that I will blow your brains out with this gun?"

"Ya'll d-don't scare me," he stammered.

All Milam could do at that point was scratch the back of his bald, shiny head. "I-I ain't never seen nothing like this before. This boy should be shitting in his drawers right about now!"

"Maybe he just too stupid to be afraid," Bryant suggested.

Milam turned in the direction of Levy and Willie. "Hey, Collins, I thought all you jigaboos was scared of your own shadows."

"I thought so too, suh."

"Well, how come this one ain't?"

"Don't know, suh,"

Milam glared down at Emmett with his .45 still pressed on the young Negro's forehead. "I guarantee ya, when we are through with this boy, he'll never sass another white woman again. Now take your clothes off!"

Emmett looked up at Milam and started pulling all of his clothes off, until he was completely nude. Milam pointed at a gin fan sitting in the back of the truck. "Go git that gin fan!" he ordered.

"I can't pick that thing up!"

"You better try," Milam said, pressing the gun down hard on his forehead.

The youngster walked over to the truck, climbed inside, and put the fan on his back. He climbed down slowly.

"Now bring it over to the river bank!" Bryant yelled at the fourteen-year-old stark naked Negro kid with a seventy-five-pound cotton gin fan on his back.

Blood started streaming down his face. As he struggled down

toward the water, he realized he was being stoned by large rocks thrown by the two grown white men, while they spit at him. He staggered to the river bank. Once he made it there, he dropped the big fan onto the ground.

Milam walked over to Emmett and again stuck the pistol back in his face. "Now I'm gonna tell you for the last time, start begging or die!"

Emmett took his time before responding. "You start begging!" he answered back.

Bryant and Milam looked at each other, not saying a word. They began waling on the young boy, hitting him in the face left and right, pounding on him as if they were trying to beat him to death. All the hatred these two white men had towards all Negroes was pouring out of them and onto Emmett.

Levy and Willie just watched in pure fear.

Emmett was on his hands and knees, coughing up blood. "You bastards don't scare me!" he said, grabbing onto his stomach in great pain.

Milam stood straight over Emmett, aiming the pistol on top of his head. "Do you think that you just as good as the white man?!" he yelled.

Emmett stood up with the gun now pressed to the side of his head. He looked both men in their eyes. "Yes I am!!" he said proudly.

Milam's eyes became glazed, and his demeanor turned even colder. "Wrong answer, nigger!" he shouted.

He let go of the trigger and shot Emmett on the right side of his head. Pieces of his brains flew out of the left side of his head and splattered on the hot ground. The young Chicago boy fell backwards like a stiff ironing board, hitting the ground hard, with his eyes wide open.

Willie Loggins was just terrified at what he had just seen. He had witnessed a lot of awful killings in Mississippi before, but this was different from all the rest. "He was only just a kid," he said, with a horrific look on his face.

Milam looked down at Emmett's sweaty, bloody, naked corpse. "A nigger is a nigger, no matter how young they are!" he screamed.

"Mr. Milam, can we just go home?" Willie asked with compassion.

"No, but what you can do is get me some barbed wire from the back of my truck, before you be lying next to this coon."

Willie hurried over to the back of the truck and grabbed a roll of long, thick barbed wire.

"Hurry up, boy, we ain't got all day!" Bryant yelled.

Willie walked up to the killers. Milam stared down at the two Negro men. "Now, the both of you, start rapping that barbed wire around that boy's neck, onto that gin fan."

"I don't know about this, Mr. Milam," Willie said in a low, nervous tone.

Milam raised his right arm up and shot off his gun three times into the air. Levy and Willie started quickly rapping the barbed wire around Emmett's neck and onto the cotton gin fan. When they were finished, Willie took off running like a track star trying to make it to the finish line.

"Come back here, boy!" Milam shouted.

"Let him go," Bryant suggested. "He ain't gonna tell nobody about this, anyways."

"He better not, if he knows what's good for him," Milam replied, wiping away the sweat that was pouring down his forehead. He turned to Levy, "Why didn't you run, boy?"

"I ain't stupid, suh," he answered in a hurry.

"You think anybody will find this boy once we drop him in this river?" Bryant turned around to ask Milam.

"There is no way in hell that anyone is gonna ever find his body, once this fan drag him down to the bottom."

"Well, I hope not, 'cause I ain't gonna go to prison over killing no spook!"

"Ain't no white man ever gonna go to prison over killing no nigger."

"I reckon not," Bryant said, his shirt drenched in sweat.

"Don't worry, little brother, once we drop this coon body in the river, no one will ever find him."

"Well, come on, let's get this done with."

Milam, Bryant, and Levy dragged the boy's battered corpse to the edge of the river bank.

"Wait!" Milam urged. "One more thang before we git rid of this boy." He pulled a sheath out of his back pocket with a sharp fish fillet knife. He knelt down on both knees. With his left hand, he pulled up Emmett's penis, and with his right hand, he started sawing on it hard and fast, until it was cut clean off. Blood splashed all around Milam's thick, sweaty neck.

"Now this will really send a message to all these filthy niggers to stay away from our white women," he said with a wicked smile.

Milam threw Emmett's penis in the river like he was tossing a rock. He wiped the bloody blade off with his own T-shirt, stuck it in the sheath and back in his pocket. "Now I feel a whole lot better!" he said, with a large grin.

Levy stood frozen, placing both hands on his knees and hunching his shoulders up.

"This boy act like he ain't never seen somebody's dick getting cut off before," Milam said jokingly.

Just seconds later, Levy vomited all over the river bank.

"I guess he haven't!" Milam laughed out loud.

Bryant was very quiet.

"What's wrong with you, little brother? We show that boy who was the boss. We put the fear of God in 'em!"

"No we didn't," Bryant said, with a serious look in his eyes.

"What you talking about, Roy?"

"No matter what we said or did to him, that boy was never afraid of us to begin with. He believed that he was just as good as us, or better."

"I know, but that's why we had to kill 'em."

"Yeah, we killed him, but why do I feel like he's the one who taught us a lesson?"

"Look, I don't wanna talk about that boy anymore. Let's just dump the body," he said in frustration.

The two white Southerners tried to lift the dead body, but the fan that was attached to Emmett made it very difficult. Milam looked at Levy. He was still bent over, with his hands still placed on both knees, sweating like crazy.

"Well, we can forget about that boy helping us. Let's try to roll him in."

Milam and Bryant rolled Emmett's body into fifty feet of dark, warm water.

The sharecropper's son, Willie Reed, had seen just about enough, and he ran a few blocks back to his shack.

CHAPTER 10

After Willie Reed gives his testimony, he starts shaking out of control.

"That was a grizzly testimony that you just shared with us, Willie," Mr. Chatham sadly nods his head.

"Since that day, I've been having nightmares about it almost ever night now."

"Was Levy Collins, who testified in this courtroom today, were he and Willie Loggins the two Negro men you saw in the back of that green pickup truck with Emmett on August the twenty-eighth?"

"Yes, suh, it was them all right."

"And you are a hundred percent sure about that?"

"No."

"Excuse me?" Mr. Chatham says with a puzzled look.

"I am a hundred and ten percent sure it was Levy Collins and Willie Loggins. I never seen them before until that morning, but I never forgot what their faces look like after that unforgettable morning."

A huge smile appears across the attorney's face. "Then I believe that's all this Court really needs to hear from you. I thank you very much, and once again, I am so glad that you did change your mind. After that strong testimony, I do believe justice will be served today. No further questions."

"You may step down now," Judge Swango tells Willie.

The young Negro looks relieved. He leaves the witness chair in a big rush and walks straight out of the courtroom back door with his head down.

"Your Honor, the two witnesses, Curtis Jones and Mose Wright, were promised before testifying today that they would be escorted out of the courtroom right before the verdict, so no harm will come to them after the trial. Miss Bradley will stay to hear the outcome of her son's case."

"Do you have someone to take them out of here?"

"Yes sir, I do, your Honor."

"Whoever they are, take them out of here, so I can get on with this trial."

The two witnesses are quickly rushed out of the courtroom by four Negro men.

"Now that is done, Mr. Carleton, you may step up to the jury with your closing arguments."

Mr. Chatham steps down, and Mr. Carleton walked over to face the jury. "Gentlemen of the jury. This Nigra boy had sexual experience before. He lived in an environment where he was very close to having sex with a white girl. Do ya'll hear me? I said a white girl! When he saw this one-hundred-'n-five-pound slim-waisted pretty white woman, Mrs. Bryant, this Nigra boy's sexual urges became so out of control, he didn't even care about what his own mama had told him about how to behave around white people in Mississippi. This Nigra boy was muscled up like a grown man. He was one of those fourteen-year-old boys who could easily be mistaken for a twenty-one-year-old man. He was a bold Nigra, too, and was not afraid of white folks at all. I was told in Chicago, where he lived, that he would say no to white storekeepers and on many occasions drew hard looks at white men and loved showing off. A picture of a white girl that he had been trying to have intercourse with, this Nigra was curious about the white women, and he attacked Mrs. Bryant in her own store. At the time of Mr. Bryant and Mr. Milam's arrest, they admitted that they took this Nigra from his uncle's cabin but just to slap him around a bit and question him about the wolf whistle incident, but later on they let him loose. As far as the body is concerned that was pulled out of the Tallahatchie River, no one knew for sure if it was the Chicago Nigra. Not even his own mama really knows!

"To convict Mr. Bryant and Mr. Milam would be a total outrage," the defense attorney continues. "The mere thought of it will have all of your forefathers rolling around in their graves!! Your Honor, the defense rests." He walks off and sits back down at the defense table with a big smile on his face. Bryant and Milam each pat him on the back.

"Mr. Chatham, are you ready for your closing arguments?" Judge Swango asks.

"Yes, your Honor, I am."

"You may approach the jury."

The district attorney walks over to the jury. He is sweating profusely. He rolls up his sleeves, and faces the jury. He looks at them, one at a time. When he finishes making eye contact, he raises his arm over his head. He speaks so loudly, it makes some people in the courtroom jump.

"They murdered this boy! And every one in this courtroom knows it. Right now, on this day, you have been given the power to demolish any native thoughts that the American citizens in this great country of ours ever had, about all Mississippians being nothing but a bunch of low-life rednecks who have no real life other than preying on and harming decent, honest, hard-working Negroes. I know that cannot be the kind of image that you want the world to have about white people in Mississippi. If you do not do what is in your hearts that is right and decent, I say shame on all of you when you wake up every morning and have to look yourselves in the mirror and not have a problem liking what's in front of you? If you let these two monsters—and that's what they are—get away with this senseless killing, it will only keep repeating itself, over and over again.

"Roy Bryant and J. W. Milam killed a fourteen-year-old boy, and to hide this dastardly, cowardly act, they forced Levy Collins and Willie Loggins to tie a barbed wire to Emmett's neck, onto a heavy gin fan. Then they dumped his gruesome corpse into the river, for the turtles and fish to nibble on. When the body was found, Emmett's teeth were knocked out, the side of his face bludgeoned in. There was a bullet hole in his right temple, and his private area was chopped off."

The district attorney pauses to prepare himself for his closure.

"This shameful blot is not just on Mississippi, but on America. Until justice has been served, by punishing these two men to the full extent of the law, no American with a conscience can really call himself a proud American. A murder was committed by the defendants you see sitting before you. I know what you are and where we are, but I beg you to put aside race tradition and prejudice and consider the facts of this case that were clearly presented. This is not an issue of Negro versus White. This is not an issue of North versus South. This is a simple issue of the law. Two men murdered a child. You have no other choice but to convict them for murder! Your Honor, I rest my case."

As the district attorney finishes his argument, Bryant and Milam show little emotion. J. W. Milam leans forward in his seat, his mouth twisted, his eyes looking at a newspaper.

Miss Bradley turns to the jury and sees that they are all smiling, laughing, and talking to one another. She is caught by an uneasy feeling. She whispers something into the ear of one of the Negro men sitting beside her at the press table. She stands up and walks out of the courtroom with a very disturbed look on her face. A tear runs across her cheek.

Judge Swango sends the jury to the deliberation room to consider their verdict. They return to the courtroom just one hour and eight minutes later. Once they are reseated, the jury foreman hands the verdict to the court clerk.

"Have the jury reached a verdict?" Judge Swango asks.

"Yes, your Honor," he answers.

"Well, what is your verdict?"

The court clerk clears his throat, then says loudly, "We the jury find the defendants, Roy Bryant and J. W. Milam, not guilty of murder!"

As soon as the verdict is announced, the district attorney slumps forward, resting his head in his hands.

The announcement triggers a loud celebration in the courtroom among the whites. Bryant and Milam shake hands, then turn and kiss their wives. Somebody hands both men cigars, and a photographer starts snapping photos to capture the racist scene.

"Order! Order! Order in my courtroom!" Judge Swango screams. He slams his gavel down several times. "Quiet down, everybody, right this second!!"

The celebration continues. Not even the Judge or the bailiff can quiet down the happy crowd.

CHAPTER 11
EPILOGUE

Several months later, after the two defendants were found not guilty of Emmett Till's murder, they were paid $4,000 by a journalist, William Bradford Hulz, to tell the story of abducting, beating, and killing Emmett Till. Roy Bryant and J. W. Milam admitted to doing all those things to Emmett, and they could tell the truth now, since they couldn't be tried for murder again. The Constitution forbids it. And no Mississippi grand jury would indict them, and they knew it. They also confessed to the journalist to throwing Emmett's body into the Tallahatchie River.

After the trial, many Negroes boycotted Roy Bryant's store, forcing him out of business. When Roy Bryant shut down his store, he could not get a job, and shortly thereafter, Bryant and his wife divorced. He went blind in 1972, and in 1994 he died of cancer.

J. W. Milam had Negroes working for him, operating his cotton pickers. After the trial, many of them stopped working for him, and he had to employ white men at higher pay. Levy Collins still continued to work for him. Milam and his wife divorced weeks later. He died of bone cancer in 1981.

Mose Wright gave lectures for the NAACP on Emmett's case, before moving to Arco, Illinois, where he farmed until his death in 1973.

Emmett's cousin, Curtis Jones, became a Chicago policeman, then retired.

Emmett's mother, Mamie Till Bradley, taught in the Chicago Public Schools for twenty-five years, until retiring. She organized several tributes to her son's memory before her death in 2003.

To the very end, Emmett still did not believe that these two white men would take his life. He was fourteen and from Chicago, and had never hurt anyone. Those funny-talking rednecks were a nightmare, but his lack of fear made Roy Bryant and J. W. Milam uncomfortable. Was he brave, or foolhardy? Ignorant, or blessed?

To be in another place, where these sick men could never touch whatever it was that enabled Emmett that day to stand his ground, to be himself, even after the last blow landed, Emmett fully understood that. Roy Bryant and J. W. Milam, who both struck with the intent to kill, were the ones who flinched that day, not Emmett.

Letter to Mamie Till Bradley

Thank you for your courage and bravely sharing your only child with the world. The heinous crime which murdered your boy, your baby, at fourteen years of age, shall never be forgotten. The news of the crime caused many people to participate in the cry for justice and equal rights, including myself. The respect I have held for you since 1955 will always live with me. You were blessed among women to carry the mantle with grace and dignity.

— *Rosa Parks*

Author's Biography

Born in 1963 in Seattle, Washington, Walter Williams Jr. has been writing since the age of ten, mostly writing plays. His first play, "A Shade of Gray," won first place in a competition, resulting in its production at the Langston Hughes Cultural Arts Center in 1990. His earliest efforts have been drama and detective novels, particularly where the subject matter is controversial.

Summary

Standing Up For Justice is about a fourteen-year-old boy who had come from Chicago to Mississippi to visit an uncle in 1955. After making a pass at a white woman, the black youth was brutally beaten, then shot. His murder and subsequent trial tell the story of how African American witnesses were courageous enough to tell the truth about what they knew of the kidnapping and killing. The murder trial also graphically exposes the ugly horrors of racism in the South.